The California Cookbook

The California Cookbook

Betty Evans

Gulf Publishing Company
Houston, Texas

For Gordon and our three children, Bob, Suzanne, and Jeanne, who continue to bring love and sunshine to my California days.

Gulf Publishing Company
Book Division
P.O. Box 2608, Houston, Texas 77252-2608

10   9   8   7   6   5   4   3   2   1

Printed in Hong Kong

Library of Congress Cataloging-in-Publication Data

Evans, Betty.
    The California cookbook / Betty Evans.
        p.   cm.
    Includes index.
    ISBN 0-88415-197-2
    1. Cookery, American—California style. 2. Cookery—California.
    I. Title.
    TX 715.2.C34E927   1994
    641.59794—dc20   94-9732
                                                    CIP

Contents

Acknowledgments

My favorite California cooking ladies, the late M.F.K. Fisher, Julia Child, and Alice Waters, for continued inspiration. Steve Hoffmann, for computer encouragement and caring proofreading. Hillary Hauser for our long standing and special friendship. My children's spouses, Susanne, Sepp, and Dana, who with the trio of grandchildren, Gordon, Evelyn, and Zachary, have helped in recipe testing. I would also like to thank my editor, Julie Starr, for all her assistance and excellent editing guidance.

About the Author

Betty Evans was born in Pasadena, California, and is a third generation Californian. Betty lives in Hermosa Beach, California, where she is a cooking teacher and food editor of the *Easy Reader*. In addition to her food interests, she is an honorary docent at the Los Angeles Museum of Natural History, California Collection chairman for the Hermosa Beach Friends of the Library, and Civic Beautification chairman for the Hermosa Garden Club. She is a past Hermosa Beach "Woman of the Year."

She is the author of *California Wine Country Cooking with Betty Evans, Honolulu Cooking with Betty Evans, San Francisco Cooking with Betty Evans, London Cooking with Betty Evans, Rome Cooking with Betty Evans, Paris Cooking with Betty Evans, Venice Cooking with Betty Evans,* and *California Cooking with Betty Evans.*

Her family, who help in testing recipes, include artist husband Gordon, son Bob, an underwater photographer and inventor living in Santa Barbara, and daughters Suzanne Evans Ackermann, an artist and chef in Zurich, and Jeanne Evans Rosen, a singer and stationery designer in Quartz Hill, California.

Foreword

I got to know Betty Evans in the late 1960s, at a time I was struggling around with writing books and magazine articles about the sea in collaboration with her son Bob, a brilliant underwater photographer. Bob was living then near the Santa Barbara waterfront in a big old building that once served as a ward for shell shock victims. In the rough-and-tumble back yard, Bob and I often sat on an old wooden bench behind a glassblower's oven, contemplating a giant clump of bamboo while encouraging each other in the very rough individual careers we had chosen to pursue.

Into this backyard arena, Betty and Gordon Evans often came with wonderful, lavish lunches and dinners that Betty had assembled in the unique and celebratory style she is now famous for. She'd come with delicious chicken and casseroles, with salads and Mexican rice and enchiladas, with lasagnas and spinach pies, beef briskets and fabulous legs of lamb. And always with bottles of delicious wine with which we'd toast each other and life and health and art. We always felt (and still feel) wonderful after one of Betty's meals, not only because of the great food, but because of the spirit that went into the making and sharing of it.

That is the best thing about Betty's cooking—the infusion of joy and spirit into the recipes. For her, fabulous cooking is not this business of trying to impress people with a lot of fancy, complicated cuisine, it is based on sharing with others a joy of life through the medium of interesting, good food that has been assembled with love and care. In this sense, Betty Evans is a Southern California version of M.F.K. Fisher, who some time ago advanced the idea that cooking is mainly a backdrop against which friends and family can sit down together and celebrate each other.

I have loved Betty Evans' cookbooks for a long time because her recipes are not only wonderful, they are trouble free and they are full of just this sort of adventure. Each little story accompanying her recipes is a gem that imparts her unique way of looking at life, as well as her impressions of the places around the world she has explored for fun and culinary offerings. Her colorful recollections are fascinating reading, and make her cookbooks far more than mere lists of ingredients and directions. How exciting for us that the focus of this book is California—with its rich coastline and offerings of seafood, its colorful wine country and inland fields of vegetables, the ethnic hearts of cities that have yielded Chinese, Italian, Mexican, Indian, and Szechwan culinary treasures. To this list, Betty has added some old family favorites that have been lovingly shared for years in the good old California backyard picnic style, and these recipes should provide some particularly good blueprints for happy gatherings.

I salute Betty for this, her latest book, and am honored to provide a few words that I hope convey the joy she has added to my life for years.

Hillary Hauser
Summerland, California

California Cooking

From Queen Calafia to Wolfgang Puck

In the beginning, Indians lived comfortably on this long strip of land bordered by the sea. Coastal Chumash ladies knew how to roast mussels and abalone over a beach wood fire. Their inland sisters made acorn concoctions and nibbled chia seeds for energy. Fables about this country drifted across to Europe. The Spanish writer Garcia Ordenez de Montalvo wrote a novel about the statuesque Queen Calafia, who rode on a gryphon and was attended by women warriors. She lived on an island overflowing with gold. The tale aroused European curiosity about this region: "West of the Indies, but to the East of Eden, lies California." This was the origin of the state's name.

The explorers Cabrillo, Sir Francis Drake, and Vizcaino sailed to the coast and found that although there was not a queen on a gryphon, California was a sunny and alluring paradise. Soon they were followed by the Spanish, who came to build missions and protected them with garrisons of soldiers. When the soldiers retired, they were given large grants of land. On these ranches, the pace was leisurely and the California tradition of fiestas and hospitality was established. Mexico won the region from Spain and life continued in much the same way.

The United States were next to possess this coveted land. During all this government shuffling, the rapidly increasing population in the state managed to eat very well. The land was fertile and bountiful. A mild climate encouraged outdoor dining and a relaxing existence.

With the gold rush in 1849, people came from all corners of the world to the state. Cities became established and were filled with restaurants of every style. Into California came the French, Italian, Japanese, Chinese, Spanish, South American, Philippine, Greek, and Russian cuisines. It was the onset of the unique California style of blending and mixing diverse cooking styles.

It is difficult to say who led the blossoming of California cuisine. Perhaps it was the late M. F. K. Fisher, who wrote *How to Cook a Wolf* during the second World War. Her simple, honest and amusing recipes are the basics of the spirit of California cooking. Mary Frances was my friend, as she was to many. I have special memories of visiting her cozy Glen Ellen home on a very stormy day. She kept the fireplace filled with madrona and oak collected from the ranch where she lived. After lunch, we sat in her front room watching dark clouds scurry across the mountains of the Jack London Ranch as we talked about cooking and life experiences. Her views on food were strictly no-nonsense. She had no patience with trendy chefs who mixed unsuitable foods, or food writers who used a lot of silly surplus adjectives. We found we were both especially amused by wine writers' usage of curious words to describe a simple red or white wine. In her last bedridden days, I came across some very whimsical descriptions of red wine characteristics and read them to her. She could not speak due to the progression of her illness, but her wonderfully expressive eyes broke into a smile. Mary Frances Kennedy Fisher leaves a remembrance of many good things, not least the heritage of unsurpassed food writing. She was the first to encourage California wineries to produce good affordable jug wines. She gave her friendship to many with unpretentious caring, and certainly was a rare state treasure.

Julia Child has had a big influence for California cooking. Julia was born in Pasadena, and will be the first to tell you that when she married, her cooking skills were minimal. A few lessons at some long gone Los Angeles cooking school taught her how to make pancakes and some other elementary dishes.

In the first years of her marriage, she moved to Paris with her husband, Paul. With her abundant energy and open California mind, Julia was ready to appreciate and absorb all that French cooking had to offer. She sensed that the American public would love French cooking if only it were presented in the right way. In her entertaining way she was able to introduce French cooking to America, and show us all how we could become creative in our own kitchens. A warm and generous lady, Julia is always ready to donate her talents to charities and needy causes.

On a quiet street in Berkeley, in the early 1970s, Alice Waters opened Chez Panisse. Alice had been a student of French cultural history and spent a year of study in France. This experience opened up a world of real food to her. She was inspired by the careful selection of ingredients, the anticipation of dining, and the enjoyment of meals consumed in a leisurely manner with lively conversation. This was what she envisioned for Chez Panisse.

I had the pleasure of meeting Alice Waters and was able to ask about her evolution as one of the world's celebrated cooks and a pioneer of California cooking. She explained that her father had had a victory garden (victory gardens were home gardens to help the war effort by feeding civilians) at their home in New Jersey. It was her delight to pick fresh vegetables with her father. Her parents made applesauce and strawberry jam. The cooking scents and the satisfaction of preparing food with your very own ingredients have always remained with her and served as a basic philosophy in her life.

Selecting the freshest and highest quality foods for Chez Panisse is Waters' pleasure and passion. Her interest extends to being supportive of farmers' markets up and down the state, and she is a fan of the gardens at the San Francisco jail. Among her favorite places to visit is the coast around Bolinas. It might seem obvious that salad is one of her preferred meals.

Wolfgang Puck was born in Austria and worked eight years in France before he came to Los Angeles to be a chef at Ma Maison. His duck salad brought him a reputation for inventive cooking. With fame came a desire for his own restaurant, so he opened Spago. It was to be a simple neighborhood place where people would drop in for a pizza and uncomplicated foods. The Hollywood crowd followed him to Spago, which remains a favorite place to dine and be seen. This could not have happened if it were not for the incredible, magically creative food. Wolf (as he is called by friends and nearly everyone else) is a friendly free spirit. Once, at Spago, he came to sit at our table and chat with our daughter Suzanne, who was working as a chef in Zurich. With a genuine open curiosity he asked all about the details of what she was cooking and about the kitchen. His employees adore him. Once I was in his Postrio restaurant in San Francisco enjoying a Hangtown breakfast when he arrived. Before he could get down the stairs cooks and waiters were running up to hug him. Wolf is a favorite with everyone.

Creating food is a passion with him. Wolf says it is like composing; first you visit the market (he likes to shop as much as he likes to cook), then you select the ingredients and finally you put them together. He says he can taste things in his head. Texture, color, and taste are his main concerns. Wolfgang Puck's restaurants are for him fantasy playgrounds that he shares with Californians.

So what is California cuisine, but a glorious mixture of fresh and beautiful ingredients combined in creative ways!

Appetizers
Little beginnings

In California, because of our diverse ethnic culture, appetizers come in many exciting flavors and forms. These little beginnings should be small and satisfying, simple and easy to eat.

Appetizers are only meant to stave off acute hunger pangs and set the mood for the meal to follow. It is important to remember that the time period for enjoying appetizers should not be extended on and on—they are only a prelude for the main courses! In this section, you will find both old traditional California standbys and current trends. Presentation is important: use attractive dishes and try some fresh garden flowers placed here and there for a garnish.

Columbus Street Marinated Olives

San Francisco is a walking city, and one of the streets I especially enjoy strolling along is Columbus Street. It is filled with captivating Italian stores. There are some selling chic Italian shoes and dresses, and others selling sleek leather furniture, but the kind I love best are the food stores. The instant you enter them, your taste buds begin to tingle. Usually, you are offered a sample taste of some special salami and cheese. Wonderful sandwiches can be made for your lunch on freshly baked, crusty Italian bread. In the glass cases are all kinds of peppers, cheeses, special meats, and various types of olives. I asked about the delicious olives in one store, and a kind employee explained to me how they are prepared.

There are extra advantages to this recipe. After you have used the olives, the marinade can be used on a salad so nothing will be wasted.

1 6-oz. can black or green pitted olives
1 garlic clove, peeled and minced
1 tsp. dried red pepper flakes
1/2 tsp. dried oregano (optional)
1/4 tsp. salt and 1/4 tsp. pepper
1/2 cup olive oil
3 T. red or white wine vinegar

Drain the olives. Mix the remaining ingredients in a jar or bowl, and stir well with a fork to blend. Add olives to the marinade and stir so they become completely coated. Refrigerate overnight.

To serve, drain the olives and place them in a pretty bowl.

Little Shrimp Toast

San Francisco's North Beach section is filled with Italian restaurants. On one of our wedding anniversaries, we flew from Los Angeles to San Francisco for a day of celebration. We decided to dine at one of the restaurants near Washington Square, the local neighborhood park.

The dining room was filled with animated diners, and the mouthwatering scents drifting around the tables were making us hungry. Our waiter suggested we begin with little shrimp toast. It was delicious, a superb mingling of Northern Italian flavors. I came home and made my own version which I have happily served for many years.

If you keep a package of frozen baby shrimp in your freezer, you can make this terrific appetizer on the spur of the moment for unexpected visitors.

Chop the shrimp medium-fine. You want a little texture, not a mush. Add the Parmesan,

1/2 lb baby bay shrimp, cooked and cleaned

1/2 cup grated Parmesan cheese

2 T. fresh lemon juice

1/2 tsp. dried or fresh thyme

1 T. minced parsley

1/2 cup mayonnaise

salt and pepper to taste

1 tsp. capers, minced

6 slices of sturdy white bread, toasted lightly and buttered

lemon juice, thyme, salt, pepper, capers, and mayonnaise. This can be prepared ahead and refrigerated.

Toast the bread, and remove crusts if desired. Spread the shrimp mixture evenly on the toast. Pat the mixture down so it looks neat and tidy. Place on a baking sheet and bake at 350° until hot and bubbly, about 8 minutes. Garnish with a little minced parsley and place on a platter. This will serve 4.

Nachos

Nachos here, nachos there, and nachos everywhere in California. They are to be found at Mexican restaurants, sporting events, office parties, airports, and as bar appetizers. The state is filled with nachos.

Nachos can be a very satisfying snack. The key to success with them is to use sturdy tortilla chips and a good quality cheese. This method for preparing nachos is simplicity itself.

Place the corn chips close together on a cookie sheet or ovenproof dish. Sprinkle the cheese over the chips. Place under the broiler until the cheese is bubbly and light

30 or more wedge-shaped tortilla chips

1-1/2 cups shredded Monterey Jack or sharpcheddar cheese

thinly sliced jalapeño peppers (canned are usually used, although fresh may be substituted. The name on the can is "Jalapeños en escabeche")

lime wedges (optional)

brown. Scatter the chopped or sliced jalapeños over the nachos according to your taste. Serve immediately, garnished with lime wedges if desired. A few drops of lime juice will add extra zap. Sometimes the corn chips are dabbed with a small amount of refried beans before the cheese is added.

Pacific Rim Rumaki

Calitornia is on the edge of the Pacific rim, where exotic flavors and influences drift across the sea. Rumaki has always been a favorite in California kitchens.

My father worked for a part of his life in public relations, and was always attending receptions for this and that. Sometimes he would take me along. What I loved best were the caterers passing trays of things to eat. It was at one of these affairs that I first tasted rumaki. I fell immediately under a sort of rumaki spell. There is something so tantalizing about the slight crunch of water chestnut, with the crispy bacon and tasty liver all hot and yummy. It was addictive, and often I would follow the person with the tray for seconds and even thirds.

Rumaki can be cooked over a low bed of charcoal, on a hibachi, or in your oven. The quantity of ingredients will depend on how many you need to serve. For each serving, use:

> *1/2 strip of bacon*
> *1/2 of a chicken liver*
> *1/2 of a water chestnut*
> *1-inch square of pineapple or papaya (optional)*
> *sprinkling of soy sauce*

Sprinkle the liver with soy sauce. Wrap the liver and water chestnut in the bacon strip. Securely hold in place with a small bamboo skewer (leaving room on top for fruit if used). Place on a metal rack (to catch the drippings) in a 400° oven, until the bacon is crisp, about 15–20 minutes. If you cook the rumaki over charcoal, turn the skewer while cooking so each side is cooked evenly.

Nan's Sicilian Caponata

My friend Nan enjoys inviting friends and family to a picnic potluck before a Hollywood Bowl concert. The combination of sharing food with friends and then listening to great music is always a happy one. One hot July evening Nan brought this terrific caponata. We all wanted the recipe immediately.

Caponata combines the tantalizing flavors of Sicily in a special treat. It keeps well in the refrigerator, and makes a perfect little snack for surprise summer drop-in visitors.

Heat oil with garlic in a heavy skillet. Dice the eggplant in pieces about 1/2″ by 1-1/2″, leaving the skin on. Sauté until golden brown. Sprinkle with the salt, then remove from the pan. In the same pan, sauté the onions, capers, and tomatoes with the remaining ingredients.

2/3 cup olive oil
1 clove of garlic, minced
1 large eggplant
2 tsp. salt
1 cup chopped onions
1/2 cup diced green pepper
1/2 cup diced celery
1 can (14–15 oz.) plum tomatoes
1 T. capers
1/2 cup sliced olives
2 tsp. dried oregano
1 tsp. basil (fresh or dried)
1/4 tsp. pepper
5 T. red or white wine vinegar
1/4 cup toasted pine nuts

Return eggplant to the pan. Simmer the mixture, uncovered, on a low flame for 20 minutes, stirring now and then. Remove from the heat. Place in a pretty bowl and refrigerate. Serve with bread or crackers. This may also be served as a salad on a lettuce leaf; the number of servings will depend on how the caponata is used.

Cook and Sing Stuffed Spinach Mushrooms

One summer my daughter Jeanne and I were trying to think of ways to earn some extra money for our various projects. We came up with the idea of creating a cooking class for the Hermosa Beach recreation program. The class would be for children, and we planned to teach them not only cooking, but a little geography as well. Jeanne was studying voice, so her contribution (as the recreation room had a piano) would be to teach them songs from the various places in the world we planned to include.

We called the class "Cook and Sing." It was fun, with 10 young boys and girls, and in an hour we had cooked and sung. This easy recipe is from the French class. Mushrooms were new to some of the children, but they all gobbled these down.

Remove stems from the mushrooms. Wash gently and carefully. Lightly pat dry with a paper towel.

12 slightly large mushrooms
1 10-oz. pkg. frozen chopped spinach
1 3-oz. pkg. cream cheese
1 whole green onion, chopped
1/4 tsp. salt
1/4 tsp. pepper
pinch of nutmeg
butter for frying (about 1/4 cup)

Cook the spinach and drain completely. You do not want any excess spinach juice as it will make the cheese mixture runny. Mash the spinach with the cream cheese, onion, and seasoning.

Fill each mushroom cavity with the mixture. Heat the butter in a frying pan. Lightly fry over a low flame until the mushrooms are hot and light brown. Serve at once as an appetizer. This may also be served with any main dish.

General Vallejo Guacamole

General Mariano Vallejo was a California "Renaissance man." He was the commander of the northern frontier when California belonged to Mexico. The general was also one of the first wine producers in Sonoma Valley. He was known for his entertaining, and had barbecue parties every week with music and dancing. Among his many interests was introducing new fruit trees to his ranchos. It is likely that these included avocados, and that his 16 daughters prepared guacamole for the parties.

Guacamole has been served in California since the earliest times. In some old cookbooks it is called "huacamole," and in others, "alligator pear spread." The secret is to prepare guacamole just before serving time. Mash it with gentle care so there are some lumps and texture; a baby food puree is not desirable.

Guacamole is usually served with tortilla chips, but it may also be mounded on a let-

2 ripe avocados, pitted and peeled
1 ripe medium sized unpeeled tomato,
  cut in tiny pieces
2 green onions, minced
1 tsp. chili powder
1 tsp. lime or lemon juice
salt and pepper to taste
1 clove garlic, peeled and finely minced
1 small Anaheim or jalapeño pepper,
  finely minced (optional)

tuce leaf and eaten as a salad. Other tasty uses are to spread it on toasted sourdough bread, or as a topping for grilled steaks. It is a Mexican tradition to serve guacamole with freshly made carnitas (roasted pork pieces; see recipe). The procedure is to spear a piece of the crispy hot meat and dip it in the guacamole. Fuerte avocados are the favored variety for guacamole, but others may be used.

Coarsely mash the avocado in a bowl. Leave some tiny lumps for texture. Blend in remaining ingredients and toss gently. Serve immediately.

Wilshire Cucumber Sandwiches

Wilshire Boulevard runs from downtown Los Angeles to the ocean in Santa Monica. It is one of the city's main arteries and a favorite street for tourists. It was named after Gaylord Wilshire, a Los Angeles pioneer. His son, Logan Wilshire, went to Occidental College with my father. The senior Mr. and Mrs. Wilshire were active in the Fabian society in England during the early part of the century, and held teas for the movement in their Hampstead Heath home.

Logan and his wife Mary lived in Brentwood and were avid gardeners. Every year in the early spring they held a Tulip party to celebrate their beautiful blooms. This was a continuation of the Wilshire tea party tradition (champagne or sherry were also offered). Mary used her mother-in-law's special recipe for cucumber sandwiches.

---

2 cucumbers, medium size, or one long 1-1/2" hothouse variety

1 T. salt (coarse preferred)

1/3 cup cider or salad vinegar

1/4 cup water

2 tsp. sugar

2 medium sized loaves of very thinly sliced white or wheat bread (sandwich size)

2 cups mayonnaise mixed with 2 tsp. lemon juice

1/4 cup butter at room temperature

My own mother enjoyed preparing these sandwiches. She helped me in my kitchen when we made refreshments for my daughter Jeanne's senior vocal recital at Northridge College. We carefully wrapped the sandwiches in damp tea towels to keep them fresh for the hour's drive from the beach to the valley. Although we had tripled the recipe, they were all quickly devoured by Jeanne's friends.

The day before you need the sandwiches, peel and thinly slice the cucumbers. Place them in a bowl with the salt, and stir so the salt will touch all the slices. Cover and refrigerate for 12 to 24 hours.

Drain the slices and pat them dry with a paper towel. Mix the vinegar, water, and sugar. Place in a bowl with the cucumber slices and let stand an hour or more. Remove the crusts from the bread. (If you feel this is wasteful, just feed them to your pets or the birds!) Arrange the bread slices on a large flat space so you have room to work. Mix the mayonnaise with lemon juice. Butter the bread slices and spread them with the mayonnaise mixture.

Drain the cucumber slices, and once more blot them dry with a towel. Place 4 pieces of cucumber on every other bread slice in the form of a cross. Cover each with another slice of bread. Cut in triangles by slicing corner to corner, crisscross. This will make 80 lovely little sandwiches. They may be wrapped in plastic, covered with a damp towel, and kept for several days in the refrigerator.

Party Salmon Dip

"What can I bring to the party?" is a very common question. This simple but classy dip is a favorite at California gatherings. Its pale pink color, with a flurry of parsley sprinkled over the top, is most appealing. Serve it with crackers or miniature rye bread slices. Celery sticks or zucchini spears may also be used.

> *1/2 lb smoked salmon*
> *1 8-oz. pkg. cream cheese (room temperature)*
> *1/4 cup sour cream*
> *1 T. lemon or lime juice*
> *1 whole green onion, minced*
> *parsley for garnish*

Cut the salmon in small pieces and combine with the remaining ingredients. This can be mixed in a blender or food processor, but I find it just as easy (and less washing up) to simply mix with a fork. Chill in a pretty bowl, and garnish with finely cut parsley.

Thailand Avocado Appetizer

The exciting diversity of immigration to California has added riches to the state's cuisine. In recent years, Thai cooking has become popular, and for good reason. It is healthy, full of titillating flavors, and fun to cook. Avocados are abundant in California, so this Thai recipe has become a favorite. It brings out the flavorful qualities and possibilities of this fruit. Serve it with sturdy potato chips or shrimp crackers (kroe poeck).

2 ripe avocados

2 T. lime juice

1 T. fresh cilantro, minced

1 red pepper, roasted, peeled, and finely diced (bottled red peppers may be used)

1/2 medium red onion, finely chopped

salt and pepper to taste

dash of hot sauce or Tabasco

Peel the avocados. Use a fork to mash them to a medium lumpy texture. Add remaining ingredients and blend together. Make this appetizer just before serving.

Extraordinary Chicken Liver Paté

I first met my friend Betty in a campground in Aix-en-Provence. She was a school teacher from California on a sabbatical leave. We found we had a lot in common besides cooking and traveling. When we had both returned to California, our friendship continued. This recipe from my friend is always popular. It is not difficult to prepare, tastes sensational, and looks very impressive.

Melt the butter in a frying pan. Sauté the onion and garlic until limp. Add the chicken livers, salt, and pepper, and fry until the livers are slightly pink inside. Add 4 tsp. of the consommé and the wine or brandy, then let cool. Add the cheeses, put the mixture in a blender, and blend until smooth.

For the aspic, heat the remainder of the consommé. Dissolve the gelatin in 1/4 cup hot water according to package instructions, and add to the consommé. Pour into a 3 to 4 cup mold or stainless steel bowl, and refrigerate until slightly thick.

You are now ready to make your own design with truffles or olives. You can have fun with this. Lay out a design on top of the aspic, or poke the things down inside it; any little creation will do. Return to the refrigerator for 20 minutes to set the design.

1/4 lb sweet butter
1 small white onion, chopped
1 clove garlic, minced
1 lb very fresh chicken livers
salt and pepper to taste
1 can chicken or beef consommé (10-1/2 oz.)
1/4 cup white wine or brandy
1 8-oz. pkg. cream cheese
1 4-oz. pkg. blue cheese
1 envelope unflavored gelatin (dissolved in 1/4 cup hot water)
truffles or black olives for garnish

Then carefully place your paté mixture on top of the aspic. Chill overnight.

To unmold, set the pan in warm water. When it is just slightly loose around the edges, turn out on a platter. Refrigerate until needed. Garnish with watercress and serve with rye bread or crackers. Of course if you're in a hurry, this can be made without the aspic; simply place the paté in pretty bowls. This will serve 8 as an appetizer.

Celery and Blue Cheese Dip

The phone rings with a request to bring something for a little nibble at some gathering. It might be a shower, office party, cocktail party, or casual dinner. This is the answer! It is quick, easy, and very good. It can be doubled or tripled as needed. Presentation is always important—take time to put the dip in a pretty glass or china bowl.

1/2 cup cream cheese (room temperature)
1/2 cup blue cheese
3 T. finely chopped celery
freshly ground black pepper to taste

Combine all ingredients thoroughly. A fork will do this quite well. Place in your pretty bowl and chill. Serve with a basket of your favorite crackers.

Devils and Angels on Horseback

Cocktail parties have always been popular with the Hollywood crowd. During the forties, "angels and devils" were all the rage. This recipe is of British origin and perhaps reflected the influence of British stars, who have always brought a blithe spirit to the movie capital. Once we had dinner in London with Val and Denis, a classic British couple. Val could hardly wait to bring me into the kitchen and show me that the prunes for her "devils" came from my home state of California. It's true—California leads the world in prune production.

"Devils" are made by simply wrapping a half strip of bacon around a pitted prune. Secure the bacon with a toothpick. Broil, turning to brown on each side, until the bacon is crisp. The devils can also be placed on a pie plate and cooked in a 450° oven until the bacon is crisp. Serve on buttered pieces of toast (the "horses") cut to fit the devils.

"Angels" are made in exactly the same way, except that instead of a prune, a small fresh oyster is used. If desired, a pinch of cayenne may be sprinkled on the angel.

Florentine Spinach Tart

There are many Italian influences in our diverse California kitchens. Spinach grows abundantly in both Italy and California, and is the basis for many delicious recipes. This spinach tart is cut in small wedges and served as a tasty appetizer, or as an additional dish for a picnic. If desired, it may be made ahead and kept refrigerated until needed. For full flavor, serve it at room temperature.

Cook the frozen spinach according to package directions. If using fresh spinach, wash it, remove the stems, and cook with just as much water as will cling to the leaves.

Cool and drain well, then squeeze dry to remove excess juice. Combine the spinach with the eggs, Parmesan, nutmeg, salt, pepper, and cheese. Rub a 10-inch pie pan with

2 10-oz. pkgs. of frozen chopped spinach (or 3 bunches fresh)

1 clove fresh garlic, peeled and minced

2 eggs, slightly beaten

1/4 cup grated Parmesan cheese

1 tsp. nutmeg

1 tsp. salt

1/2 tsp. pepper

1 cup (8 oz.) ricotta or small curd cottage cheese

1/4 cup pine nuts (shelled)

1 T. olive oil

olive oil. Spread the mixture evenly around the pan, and top with pine nuts. Bake at 350° for 20 minutes. Cool on a rack, and cut in wedges to serve.

This tart can also be made in two 9-inch pans but it will not be as high.

Elegant Endive Garnished with Caviar

2 Belgian endives
2 T. black caviar
2 T. red caviar

My first experience with endive was in Paris, where everyone in the city seemed to be eating it. Endive was sold from a cart on my food marketing street, Rue Lepic. I was told it was grown in caves in Belgium. These crunchy delicate little leaf bundles, so specially grown, intrigued me. I began using endive in salads and filling the leaves with little dabs of things for appetizers. When I returned to California, endive was found only in specialty markets, but it has since become popular here and is now easily available. The glossy pale-colored leaves of endive, arranged on a plate with a touch of glistening caviar, make an impressively beautiful combination.

Separate the endive leaves, and pick out the most perfect. (Any endive not used can be added to a salad.) Arrange on a plate with the tips facing outwards. Usually about 6 leaves per person is ample.

Divide the caviar among the leaves. Just place a dab on the inside of each leaf. This should serve 4.

Melons, Figs, Papaya, and Pears with Prosciutto

This is one of the simplest and most refreshing beginnings to any dinner. Californians have borrowed the idea from the traditional Italian antipasti offerings, using the state's special ripe fruits.

To use ripe melons (cantaloupe, honeydew, Persian, casaba, or Crenshaw), peel them and cut into crescent-shaped slices. Drape a thin slice of prosciutto on each slice. Or, you might prepare melon balls and attach them with toothpicks to little slices or cut squares of prosciutto.

Figs should be split in half, with the ham laid over the figs. Papaya is peeled, seeded, and arranged in slices in an attractive design on a plate; the prosciutto is then laid on top of the slices.

Pears should be peeled, cut in wedges, and sprinkled with some lemon juice to avoid discoloration. As with the melons, the prosciutto is then draped over the wedges. Pears and prosciutto is certainly one of the most delicious combinations.

The amount of prosciutto required for this appetizer will vary, but usually 1/4 lb will be sufficient. Do not be alarmed by the price of prosciutto; it is sliced very thin and will not cost as much as you might think. In Italy, freshly ground black pepper is often served with these antipasti.

Hungarian Cheese Spread

One of California's most popular Hungarian characters was Agoston Haraszthy, a nobleman whose travels led him with his family to Sonoma. In 1857, he planted grapes on the site of the present Buena Vista Vineyard. This enterprising man was then able to obtain a commission from the California legislature to gather information from Europe about wine producing methods. From that trip, he brought one hundred thousand grape cuttings back to Sonoma. This adventurous man became known as "the father of California wine." His palatial home was the scene of many social gatherings renowned for excellent and bountiful food. This cheese spread from Hungary is still popular at California parties.

8 oz. cream cheese (at room temperature)

1/4 cup butter (at room temperature)

1 T. minced capers

1 T. caraway seed

3 T. minced chives or green onion tops

1 T. Dijon-style mustard

1 T. paprika

1/4 tsp. salt

1/4 cup sour cream

1/2 tsp. anchovy paste, or 2 minced anchovies (optional)

Cream the butter and cream cheese together. Add remaining ingredients and blend. Store in small bowls in the refrigerator. Serve with crackers or small rounds of rye bread. Let stand at room temperature for 20 minutes for easier spreading.

Celery with Walnut Cream Cheese

It is a natural idea to pair two of the state's prolific crops for a most flavorful combination. This could not be more simple to make; it takes only a few minutes. This is a healthy and very pretty appetizer.

Place the butter and cheeses in a bowl, and mash together. Spread the mix in the chan-

1 T. butter (at room temperature)
1 T. blue cheese
1 3-oz. pkg. cream cheese
2 T. walnuts, chopped and lightly toasted
6 stalks celery, cleaned and cut in 4-inch lengths

nels of the celery. Sprinkle walnuts on top. A few nasturtiums on the plate will make an attractive garnish.

Easy California Olive Spread

In California mission gardens, you can see marvelous, ancient, gnarled olive trees. Missionaries brought these trees from Spain, and olives and olive oil were a main ingredient in the mission fathers' cuisine. This recipe, reflecting these early flavors, is delightful and easy to prepare.

Melt the butter in a small frying pan. Add the onion, and cook until soft and limp. Do not brown.

Place the cream cheese in a bowl. Add the butter-onion mixture. Cream with an electric mixture or by hand.

1/4 lb sweet butter

1 medium white onion, finely chopped

1 8-oz. can of green or black pitted olives

1 8-oz. pkg. cream cheese (room temperature)

1/2 tsp. chili powder

Drain and coarsely chop the olives. Add the olives and the chili powder to the creamed mixture. Blend well. Place in a serving bowl and chill.

Serve with crackers, melba toast, or sturdy tortilla chips. This will keep in the refrigerator for a week.

San Francisco Celery Victor

Celery Victor is one of California's traditional dishes, created several decades ago by Victor Hirtzler of the Saint Francis Hotel in San Francisco. It can be served as a first course or in place of a salad.

Celery does deserve to be more popular. In the Middle Ages, it was recommended for "calming irritated states of mind." Today, it is still known as a nerve calmer. Celery is always available, moderate in price, and low in calories.

Wash and trim the celery, and cut into 5-inch stalks. Place the broth in a saucepan. Drop in the stalks. Simmer covered just until tender, about 25 minutes. Do not overcook. Cool the celery in the broth. This delicious celery-flavored broth may be saved for later use as soup.

1 medium bunch of celery

3 cups chicken broth (homemade or canned)

1 cup French dressing (recipe follows)

salt and pepper to taste

fresh red pepper (or canned or bottled pimiento) for garnish

Prepare a basic French dressing by combining 2/3 cup olive oil with 1/3 cup wine vinegar. Season with salt and pepper to taste, and mix well with fork.

Remove the celery from the broth and place in a bowl. Pour the dressing over it. Chill for several hours or overnight.

To serve, remove celery from dressing. Place 3 stalks on a small serving plate. Spoon some of the dressing on each serving. Garnish with a few strips of pimiento or red pepper in an "X" design. Let stand at room temperature for about 15 minutes before serving, for the fullest flavor. This will serve 4.

Rumaki Party Spread

This is a handy alternate version of rumaki. It has all the flavors of traditional rumaki, but may be made ahead.

Melt the butter. Sauté the livers and onion until the onion is limp and the livers slightly pink (overcooking liver will make it tough). Mash with a fork—blenders or food processors puree excessively. Add the remaining ingredients and blend. Place in a bowl and refrigerate at least an hour. This will keep well in the refrigerator for several days. Garnish with a few cilantro leaves, and serve with sesame crackers or shrimp chips.

1 lb chicken livers, each cut in half

1/2 cup sweet butter

1 small onion, diced

dash of cayenne pepper or hot pepper sauce

6 slices of bacon, cooked and crumbled

1 8-oz. can of water chestnuts, drained and coarsely chopped

salt and pepper to taste

3 T. soy sauce

Party Taco Tart

Parties in California are usually casual and often spur-of-the-moment ideas. One evening, my friend Fran invited me over for wine and appetizers with some friends. It was the first time I had tasted taco tart, and before I could finish my glass of wine I somehow had devoured half the tart. This is one of those tasty things you can't stop eating.

Spread the beans in a 10″ or 12″ pie pan or bowl and smooth the top. Spread the sour cream over the beans. Sprinkle half the taco seasoning over the sour cream.

Spread the avocado, then the salsa. Sprinkle onions over the salsa and layer the cheese over this. Add the remaining half of the taco seasoning on top of the cheese. Sprinkle the black olives next, followed by the tomatoes.

1 17-oz. can refried beans
1 8-oz. carton of sour cream
1 pkg. of taco seasoning (1-1/4 oz.)
*1 medium sized avocado, mashed,
    seasoned with salt and pepper to taste*
1 7-oz. can green chili salsa
2 green onions, finely chopped
2 cups grated cheddar or jack cheese
1 2.2-oz. can chopped olives, drained
2 medium sized tomatoes, diced
cilantro for garnish
tortilla chips

Cover and refrigerate for an hour or more, so the flavors mellow. Before serving, garnish with fresh cilantro. Serve with a good sturdy tortilla chip that can dip down through the layers without falling apart!

Spinach-Stuffed Hard Boiled Eggs

I first tasted these eggs at an Easter picnic in a friend's back yard that was filled with spring flowers. The look of a mixed yellow and green filling sitting in the white halves of the eggs is quite lovely, and the mingled flavor of spinach and eggs is very appealing. Serve these on a platter garnished with some fresh flowers. This appetizer is popular at potluck parties.

Cook the spinach. Drain and squeeze dry. This is important as you do not want any excess spinach juice in this dish.

Carefully shell the eggs and slice them in half lengthwise. Separate the yolks from the whites. Mash the yolks with spinach, mayon-

12 eggs, hard-boiled

1 10-oz. pkg. chopped frozen spinach (or 1 bunch of fresh spinach, cooked, chopped, and drained)

salt and pepper to taste

1/4 cup mayonnaise

2 T. olive oil

2 T. grated Parmesan cheese

salt and pepper to taste

naise, oil, cheese, salt, and pepper. Fill each egg white half with the yolk mixture. Try to do this neatly so that the white of the egg does not have the filling dribbling over it; the beauty of this dish is the pristine look of the white against the green-yellow color. Chill, covered with foil or plastic wrap, until serving time.

Vineyards Stuffed Grape Leaves

California wine makers make other things besides wine. Most are excellent cooks and enjoy entertaining. In the spring, when grape leaves are young and tender, this is a popular appetizer. The filling is non-meat and is a very refreshing prelude to a springtime dinner. Of course, dolmas, as they are called in the Middle East, can be made any time of the year using preserved bottled leaves.

If fresh leaves are used, drop them, a few at a time, into a simmering pot of water and blanch for 3 minutes. Remove with a slotted spoon. Place at once into a bowl of ice water to prevent further cooking, then remove and drain on paper towels. If preserved leaves are used, rinse carefully in cool water. Stems should be snipped off either the fresh or preserved leaves.

In a saucepan, heat 3 T. of the oil. Cook onion until limp, then add rice and cook just until the grains are glossy (about 2 minutes). Add water and cover. Cook over a low

40 medium sized fresh grape leaves
   (bottled may be substituted)
1 cup chopped onion
6 T. olive oil
1/3 cup uncooked long-grain rice
3/4 cup water
salt and pepper to taste
2 T. pine nuts
2 T. currants
1 T. fresh chopped mint leaves (optional)
1/4 cup white wine or water
lemon wedges or yogurt for garnish

flame for about 15 minutes. The rice should be tender, but not mushy.

Heat 1 T. of the oil in a small pan. Brown the pine nuts just until barely golden. Add to rice with currants and mint (if used). Season with salt and pepper to taste.

Line the bottom of a heavy 2- or 3-quart casserole with 10 of the leaves. Arrange the remaining leaves, dull side up, on a flat

(continued on next page)

(continued from previous page)

working surface (a bread board works nicely). Make sure any stem ends are snipped off.

Place 1 T. of the filling in the center of each leaf. Fold the stem end of the leaf over the stuffing. Fold left side of leaf toward the center. Repeat with right side. Now, starting at the stem end, roll the leaf into a little sausage-like shape. Do not roll too tightly, as the filling will expand slightly.

Stack, with seams down, snugly in the casserole. Sprinkle with the remaining olive oil and wine. Cover and simmer over a very low flame for 45 minutes. Uncover, cool to room temperature, and carefully remove from the casserole. Arrange in an attractive design on a platter. Garnish with lemon wedges. Yogurt may be drizzled on top or served in a bowl on the side. This will make 30 dolmas. They may be refrigerated, but are at their best served at room temperature.

Soups

Hot and Cold

Soups, in many ways, fit perfectly into the California culinary scene. One of my fondest soup memories is from San Francisco. The day was windy and white cloud puffs drifted across an incredibly blue sky as my husband Gordon and I had our first taste of artichoke soup in a Nob Hill hotel. The soup was a specialty of the hotel and every fragrant bite of it was pleasing. The impeccably dressed waiter saw our obvious enjoyment and offered us a soup refill. We quickly accepted.

Another memory recalls a snowy campground in Yosemite National Park, a few days before Christmas. Our family built a large campfire with the fallen wood we had collected all afternoon (this is permitted). The wood was damp, but we had carried dry kindling from home and soon had a roaring fire going. A reserved bottle of red wine was opened. I took the frozen minestrone from the ice chest and slowly heated it over a grill in a corner of the fire. French bread was wrapped in foil to heat, and soon the soup dinner was ready.

Summers can be very hot in Santa Barbara. Chilled gazpacho with a pitcher of white sangria makes a perfect summer soup luncheon there, outdoors on a shady patio in sight of the Figueroa Mountains.

In my early married days we lived in New York while my husband attended the Art Students League on the GI Bill. My sister-in-law Grace lived with us too. She was studying opera. I had a rather low-paying job with the Ice Capades in Rockefeller Center. Our rent was high and our food budget tiny. The three of us used to share a can of Campbell's Bean with Bacon soup, along with sandwiches and tea for dinner. It filled us in the warming way that only soup does.

Yosemite Park Minestrone

Yosemite National Park is one of the wonders of our world. Its unsurpassed beauty offers visitors changing moods for each day and hour of the year. My favorite time is winter, when the summer crowds are gone and there is snow, high white clouds, and mist. In the winter, Yosemite Falls is full, and this cascade of over 2000 feet can be heard throughout the park. It is exciting to climb up a trail and stand in front of it. My son says it gives you healthy ions.

Our family likes to enjoy our dinner in a campground, even in chilly weather. I make this minestrone at home, and freeze it to take to the park. It then can be warmed on a campfire and enjoyed in the midst of a winter wonderland.

3 qts. water

1 onion, chopped

1–2 lb beef shank bone, or any other soup bone

3 ribs celery, diced

1 cup white great northern or navy beans

2 cloves of garlic, minced

1 14-oz. can whole tomatoes

1/4 cup fresh parsley, snipped

1 tsp. dried thyme

salt and pepper to taste

2 medium sized zucchini, diced

1 10-oz. pkg. frozen peas

1 10-oz. pkg. frozen lima beans

1 15-oz. can garbanzo beans

1/2 cup spaghetti (broken in 1-inch lengths)

Parmesan cheese and minced parsley for garnish

In a large soup pot place the onion, garlic, celery, beans, beef shank, tomatoes, parsley, thyme, salt and pepper. Simmer, covered, until the beans are tender (about an hour and 15 minutes). Remove the cover and add the zucchini, peas, limas, garbanzos, and spaghetti. Cook until the vegetables are tender, about 15 minutes. This is a thick soup—minestrone means "big soup!" If you wish a thinner soup, add some extra liquid. A dash of red or white wine always enhances the flavor.

Before serving, discard the bone, mince the meat, and return it to the soup. Garnish each bowl with Parmesan cheese and minced parsley. This will serve 10. If you do not have 10 for dinner, freeze in two 5-person portions. Remember, Yosemite is open every day of the year!

Nob Hill Artichoke Soup

Nob Hill is one of the steepest, most exhilarating hills in the city of San Francisco. The name came from the word "nabob," which means anyone of great wealth, because the hill was once lined with the grand mansions of the nouveau riche. Today it is the location of some of the city's finest hotels. Artichoke soup is typical of Nob Hill hotel cuisine.

Place the artichokes with chicken broth in a large saucepan. Cover and simmer 10 minutes or until the hearts are tender. A cup and a half of fresh trimmed hearts may be substituted for the frozen, but will take a little longer to cook.

1 9-oz. pkg. frozen artichoke hearts, or 1 14-oz. can artichoke hearts. If using canned, drain and cut each piece in half.

3 cups chicken broth

1/4 cup white wine

1/2 cup half-and-half

salt and pepper to taste

Parmesan cheese or toasted grated hazelnuts

Place the mixture in a food processor and blend to a smooth texture, then return to the pan. Add half-and-half, salt, and pepper. Heat to serving temperature, and serve with your choice of garnishes. This will make four servings. Served cold, this soup is perfect for lunch or supper on a hot summer's day.

Grant Avenue Egg Flower Soup

If you enjoy the adventures of exploring a city, Grant Avenue in San Francisco's Chinatown is the place to be. Wander along this colorful street and discover Chinese markets and souvenir stores. Peek into the restaurants where Chinese cooks perform food miracles in woks. Tourists are often timid when ordering Chinese meals, and stick to the fixed price 4 or 5 item menu, but a little spirit of adventure will bring you delightful surprises.

This delicate and tantalizing soup is offered in many restaurants. It is easy to make at home while you recall happy memories of Chinatown.

Heat the broth to simmering, and add the soy sauce. Blend the water and cornstarch to make a smooth mixture. Add to soup and simmer a few minutes. If you want any

4 cups chicken broth (homemade or canned)

1 tsp. soy sauce

1 T. cornstarch mixed with 1/4 cup water

2 eggs

2 T. finely minced green onion tops

optional: sliced water chestnuts, fresh mushroom slices, bamboo shoots, diced chicken, or diced pumpkin

of the optional ingredients, add them at this time.

Mix the eggs lightly with a fork. Pour slowly, in a thin stream, into the soup, stirring as you pour to make the "egg flower" drops. Serve at once garnished with green onions. This will serve 4.

When you are in Chinatown, purchase some Chinese soup bowls and spoons for serving this soup at home. They are handy for many uses and make a nice remembrance of your Chinatown adventures.

Portuguese Bean Soup

Portuguese bean soup is a favorite in Hawaii. The Hawaii-California connection has had a strong influence on the cuisine of this state. There are great travel packages from the West Coast to Hawaii so many Californians enjoy visiting the Aloha state. One of our friends who lives in Hawaii shared this recipe with me. It is from one of the original Portuguese families that settled in Oahu.

Cover beans with water and soak overnight. Drain, place in a soup pot, and cover with 2 quarts of water. Add onion, ham hock, salt, and pepper. Cover and simmer for one hour, stirring now and then.

Remove cover and take out the ham hock. Add tomato sauce and celery. Remove ham from bones and dice. Return to the pot and

1 lb dried red or kidney beans (or a combination of both)

1 medium onion, sliced

1 medium sized ham hock

salt and pepper to taste

1 8-oz. can of tomato sauce

2 stalks of celery, diced

2 medium sized potatoes, peeled and diced

1 small cabbage, chopped or thinly sliced

1-1/2 cup uncooked small elbow macaroni

1/2 lb Portuguese or any hot sausage, thinly sliced

simmer uncovered for 20 minutes. Add remaining ingredients. Continue to cook for an additional 30 minutes. If the soup is too thick for your taste, thin with water or white wine. Garnish with minced parsley or watercress. This will serve 6–8.

Creamy Clam Chowder

Up and down the California coast there are many small, cozy fish restaurants. Their menus feature fresh local fish, and often the dinner will begin with a cup of clam chowder. The chowder will warm your stomach and is a good beginning to a fish dinner. This flavorful chowder is easy to make at home and is a perfect main dish for a cool evening dinner.

Melt the butter in a saucepan. Add the onion and bacon, and cook together until light brown. Add the juice from the can of clams, the wine and diced potatoes (if you are using fish, add an extra 1/2 cup liquid—water, wine, etc.). Add salt and pepper to taste. Cover and cook until potatoes are tender.

2 tsp. butter

2 slices of bacon or salt pork, diced

1 onion, peeled and chopped

3 cups raw potatoes, peeled and diced

1 cup dry white wine

1 7-oz. can of chopped clams, or 1 cup fresh diced clams (fish may also be used)

1 cup milk

1 cup half-and-half

salt and pepper to taste

Remove cover and add clams (or fish), milk, and cream. Heat thoroughly, stir well, and serve. A little sprinkle of parsley or chopped red bell pepper adds a colorful touch. This will serve 4.

Summer Senegalese Soup

Cold soups have always been popular in California, because of our many months of warm weather. They taste refreshing and can be easily made in the cool morning hours. This soup, with its pale yellow colors and mixture of slightly exotic flavors, is always a treat.

Melt the butter. Add the flour and curry powder, and blend together. Slowly add the broth and cook one minute.

Mix the cream or half-and-half with the egg yolks. Gently add to the broth while stirring, and cook one minute. Stir in the chicken. Add salt and pepper to taste. Refrigerate until serving time.

> *1 cup minced or finely shredded cooked chicken breast*
> *3 cups chicken broth*
> *1 cup half-and-half or light cream*
> *2 T. butter*
> *2 T. flour*
> *1 T. curry powder*
> *2 egg yolks*
> *salt and pepper to taste*
> *chopped peanuts and chives for garnish*

To serve, garnish with peanuts and chives. This will make four bowls. Of course if the fog should roll in and the day become cool, this soup is also delicious served hot.

La Purisma Concepcion Mission Albondigas Soup

Many visitors to California enjoy visiting the chain of missions from San Diego to Solano. La Purisma Mission, founded in 1787, is one of the largest and best-restored. Mission crafts are well displayed and often demonstrated. There is room to picnic and some atmospheric hiking trails.

Albondigas soup was a favorite of the mission cuisine. This is an easy soup to prepare ahead and have ready in your refrigerator. You will only need some tortillas or bread with a green salad for an easy soup dinner.

Heat the oil in a frying pan. Lightly brown the onion and garlic. In a bowl, break the bread into the beaten egg and mix together. Add the meat, onion, garlic, oregano, cornmeal, chile, salt and pepper. Make meatballs about the size of a walnut from this mixture.

1 lb lean ground beef (or 1/2 lb ground beef and 1/2 lb ground pork)

1 slice white bread

1 egg, slightly beaten

1 onion, finely minced

1 clove of garlic, peeled and minced

1 T. vegetable oil

1/2 tsp. oregano

1/2 cup white or yellow corn meal

salt and pepper to taste

1 fresh green Anaheim chile, chopped finely

2 qts. chicken or beef stock (can be homemade or canned)

1 8-oz. can tomato sauce

Heat the stock with the tomato sauce. Drop meatballs into the soup. Cook uncovered for 25 minutes. This will serve 6. Place 3 meatballs in each soup bowl. If any are left over they make tasty sandwiches.

San Francisco's French Onion Soup

The French came to San Francisco to join the search for gold. Soon they became disenchanted with the menial work in the mining fields and realized that the real gold could be found in serving good French food to hungry miners. They were among the first to open restaurants in San Francisco, and French onion soup is now a traditional part of the California menu.

4 T. butter

2 T. peanut or olive oil

6 medium white or yellow onions, thinly sliced

salt and pepper to taste

1 T. flour

2 qts broth—this may be homemade or canned, chicken or beef

1 cup dry white wine

6 buttered slices of French bread

4–5 T. grated Parmesan cheese

Melt the butter and oil in a soup pot. Add the sliced onions. Stir around to blend. Cover and cook over a low flame for 20 minutes, giving a stir now and then. Uncover, stir in salt, pepper, and flour. Add broth and wine. Simmer uncovered over a low flame for 40 minutes.

Sprinkle the cheese on top of buttered bread slices. Place under broiler and toast until lightly brown. Ladle soup into bowls and top with bread. This will serve 6.

Many restaurants serve onion soup in nice brown bowls that can be put directly under the broiler and served with the cheese and bread mixture running over and down the sides. If you own a set of these ovenproof bowls, by all means use them, but for the average home soup cook this other method works well and you do not have to wash those gooey bowls.

Egyptian Lentil Soup

What is an Egyptian soup doing in a California cookbook? There has always been a mystique about Egypt in California. Architecture in Hollywood has Egyptian influences. Museums feature Egyptian exhibits. Costume shops feature Cleopatra costumes and there are even Egyptian restaurants.

Lentils have been grown and used as a staple food in Egypt for over 5000 years. Lentil soup is a traditional menu choice in Egypt.

Cover the lentils with eight cups of water. Add the onion, garlic and seasonings. Cover and simmer, stirring now and then, until lentils are tender (about an hour). Puree the soup in a blender or food processor, or push through a colander. You want a smooth mixture.

1 pkg. lentils (12 or 14 oz.)
1 onion, chopped
2 cloves of garlic, minced
1 T. cumin powder
1 T. curry powder
salt and pepper to taste
croutons
lime slices

Reheat the soup in a pot. You may wish to thin it with a little white wine; although this is not in the Moslem tradition, it adds a zap to the soup.

Garnish with the croutons. Serve with a wedge of lime to squeeze into the soup. This soup is rather muddy in color, so a few croutons sprinkled on the top will improve its appearance.

Green Flecked Watercress Soup

Beautiful green watercress grows freely along many California streams, and has always been a favorite in California salads and garnishes. Watercress gives a lovely nippy flavor to soup. Try this soup for a light summer dinner, with white wine and hot crusty French rolls.

Combine potatoes, water, onion, salt, and pepper in a soup pot. Cover and simmer for about 40 minutes or until the potatoes are quite tender. Break up the potatoes with a fork or potato masher so you have a crumbly texture. Do not use a blender or processor, as this will only produce a mush.

1 lb potatoes, peeled and sliced (white rose recommended)

4-1/4 cups water

1 onion, diced

salt and pepper to taste

1 bunch of watercress, washed and chopped

1 cup milk (or half-and-half)

1/4 cup white wine

Add the watercress and simmer with soup mixture for 5 minutes. Add the milk (or half-and-half) and wine. Stir to blend, and heat to serving temperature. Do not boil. This will serve 5. If you prefer to serve this soup cold, chill it in the refrigerator and stir before serving.

Roman Chicken Rag Soup with Spinach
(Stracciatella alla spinaci)

Roman roads lead everywhere, even to California. Italian families usually became involved in growing food or operating restaurants when they arrived in California. This classic recipe came with them and makes good use of the state's bountiful spinach crop. If you need a nourishing soup that will revive spirits after an illness or a long night of partying, this is the perfect choice.

The whimsical name "little rags" is an imaginative description of the flecks of eggs in the soup.

6 cups clear chicken broth (homemade or canned)

1/4 cup white wine (optional)

3 eggs, lightly beaten

salt and pepper to taste

1 bunch fresh spinach (or one 10-oz. pkg. frozen leaf spinach)

3 T. Parmesan cheese

Heat the broth to simmering, adding wine if used. Lightly beat the eggs with a fork in the bowl. Very slowly and carefully pour the eggs into the soup, stirring constantly with a fork. In a minute or so you will have the "little rags." Cook the spinach and squeeze dry to avoid excess green juice. Add to the soup and stir with the "rags." This will serve 6.

Alambique Spanish Gazpacho

California has many close ties with Spain. The Spanish were the state's earliest settlers, bringing in their missions and many culinary influences.

In Madrid, there is a renowned cooking school and culinary store named Alambique, which is popular with both Spanish and Americans. The school's dynamic proprietor, Clara Maria de Amezua, shared this recipe with me.

Cut into small pieces the bread, tomatoes, cucumber, and bell pepper. Add the water, vinegar, salt, pepper and garlic. Set aside to marinate for one hour in a cool place.

Puree the marinated mixture in a blender or food processor until it is smooth. Pour in the oil and blend an additional minute. Place in a large serving bowl. Add a few ice cubes. Keep in refrigerator until well chilled.

2 cloves garlic, mashed
1 small loaf Italian-style white bread
3 to 3-1/2 lb fresh ripe tomatoes, peeled and seeded
half a medium sized cucumber
1 green bell pepper
4 cups water
1/2 tsp. freshly grated pepper
3 T. vinegar
1 tsp. salt
8 T. olive oil

Garnish:
half a cucumber, diced
half a green bell pepper, diced
1 cup of croutons

Serve in individual bowls. Put the garnish in a separate bowl, passing it so each person can add their own. This will serve 6–8. It may be kept for several days in the refrigerator.

Fisherman's Wharf Cioppino

Several decades ago, San Francisco was a major fish market. While the fishermen were sorting the day's catch for the market, it was a tradition among them to cook a fish soup on the decks of their ships. Accounts of these days recall the tantalizing smells coming from the wharf. The word "cioppino" supposedly evolved from the fisherman's cry, "Chip in, o!" The fishermen would add whatever was in their bounty to the simmering pot. This is still the best way to prepare this dish, by including only whatever is fresh and in season. Use this recipe simply as a basic guideline for cioppino.

Cioppino makes a wonderful company dinner. Have your guests serve themselves from the soup pot. Provide some fresh sourdough bread to wipe up the juices. A bottle of red wine and big napkins are usually included with cioppino.

In a large soup pot, heat the olive oil over a medium flame. Add the onion, green pepper,

1/4 cup olive oil
1 medium onion, chopped
1 green pepper, chopped
2 fresh garlic cloves, minced
2 cups red or white wine
salt and pepper to taste
1 bay leaf
1/2 tsp. thyme
2 28-oz. cans solid pack, crushed, or diced tomatoes
1 lb halibut or other firm fish, cut in 1-inch cubes
12 fresh clams in shell, scrubbed, or one 6-1/2 oz. can chopped clams
1/2 lb peeled and deveined medium shrimp
1/2 lb scallops or fresh crab
fresh minced parsley for garnish

and garlic. Stir and cook just until limp. Add wine, seasonings, and tomatoes. Mix together. Simmer uncovered over a low flame for

(continued on next page)

(continued from previous page)

30 minutes. Break up any large tomato pieces. This much may be done ahead and refrigerated.

To the simmering stock add the fish and clams. Cook for 15 minutes, covered. Uncover and add the remaining ingredients. Continue to simmer for another 10 minutes. Garnish with parsley and serve from the pot. This will make 4 generous helpings.

Fish and Seafood

New and Traditional Recipes from California's Waters

The coast of California stretches nearly 900 miles. The state has long rivers, meandering streams, and deep lakes. Swiftly swimming fish live in all these waters. Fishing is an important state industry, and seafood restaurants are very popular.

Once our family was camping in Northern California. We passed a small fish market on the coast. Draped across the store front was a big banner announcing fresh salmon. Of course, we stopped and purchased the salmon, caught early that morning. Back at the campground I cooked it over coals. It was so fantastic. We simply squeezed a lemon over it. This was a fish lesson for me, to always remember that there is nothing as wonderful as truly fresh fish. I remember walking around the large fish market in Venice. There was only the scent of the sea.

This is the way a fish market should be. Pay attention to where you purchase your fish and only buy the freshest.

Pier and barge fishing are popular in California. My father at one time did publicity for the Olympic fishing barge anchored off Hermosa Beach. Part of his compensation was free passes for the barge. The big catch always seemed to be local mackerel. I was a toddler and loved to play with the wiggling mackerel. Their slippery skins were a luminous green and they were fun to touch. Our family ate this fish prepared with onions and a little wine to help improve the rather strong taste. It is not the most perfect eating fish, but food was food during the Depression. We had to be careful not to accidentally swallow a fish bone. Mackerel is still one of the most frequently caught pier fish today.

Because of health concerns, many people in California are eating more fish now than in former years. The recipes in this chapter offer new ideas and variations for your fish cooking cuisine.

Summer and early fall are albacore season in California. Albacore is a tuna-like fish that is a favorite for California dinners. One day we were walking home with friends from a day at the beach and we passed a fisherman who was pulling into his driveway with a catch of fresh albacore. We asked him about his fishing expedition and after the story he mentioned he had too many for his family. Would we like some? This is an offer that cannot be resisted and we carried two home in a big plastic bag. They were cleaned in my kitchen, cut into steaks, and baked with white wine. Our friends stayed for dinner.

I have friends who are trout fishermen. They do it for the sport, and carefully return the fish to the gurgling streams. I like to keep the ones we catch, and eat them grilled fresh over a campfire.

Sea Bass in an Easy Wine Sauce

Wine adds a magical zest to many fish recipes. This method of marinating and then completing the cooking with the same marinade is a popular technique in California. This dish is usually served hot, but on hot summer days it is equally delicious chilled and served on a bed of shredded lettuce.

Mix olive oil, lemon juice, garlic, salt, pepper, and bay together. Cut the fish in 4 serving pieces, place in a shallow glass or china dish, and cover with the marinade. Let the fish rest in this marinade in a cool place for 30 minutes, turning once for absorption of flavors.

Remove fish from marinade and set the marinade aside. Pat the fish dry with paper towels. Dust with flour on both sides. Heat oil and butter in a frying pan. Fry the fish

2-1/2 lb fresh sea bass, halibut, or any other firm fish
1/4 cup olive oil
juice from one medium lemon
2 fresh garlic cloves, peeled and minced
salt and pepper to taste
1 bay leaf
flour
1/2 cup white wine
2 T. butter and 2 T. olive oil for frying
parsley and lemon wedges for garnish

on one side until it is golden brown, then turn it and fry the remaining side. Lower the flame and add the marinade and wine. Cover and cook over a low flame until the fish is cooked, about 10 minutes, depending on fish. Discard the bay leaf. Serve the fish with the pan wine sauce, garnished with lemon wedges and minced parsley. This will make 4 servings.

Chinatown Shrimp Butterflies

The Chinese helped to build California, and in the process gave us a rich culinary legacy. Up and down the state, the many Chinatowns are always popular and crowded with restaurant customers.

Shrimp butterflies are a favorite with everyone. With a little of your imagination, the shrimp really do look like pink butterflies. They are accompanied by a bowl of hot mustard and one of ketchup. The shrimp is held in your hand and gently dunked in the two sauces. Each bite should be slowly savored.

Shell the shrimp, keeping the tail intact. With a sharp knife, split the shrimp and gently press open and devein. The idea is that by keeping the tail the shrimp will have a "butterfly" look. Mix soy sauce, sherry and ginger together in a bowl. Marinate the shrimp in this mixture for an hour. Salt and pepper are usually not needed, as the soy contains salt.

1 lb of large shrimp (about 16 count)
2 T. soy sauce
2 T. sherry
1 T. finely minced fresh ginger
1/2 cup cornstarch
1 egg, beaten
cracker meal or fine bread crumbs
peanut or other cooking oil for frying
ketchup and hot mustard for dipping

Drain the shrimp. On a piece of waxed paper (or a plate) place the cornstarch, and on another, about one cup of meal or crumbs. Beat the egg in a bowl. Dip the shrimp in the cornstarch, dunk in the egg and lastly roll in the crumbs. The amount of dry ingredients may vary so use more or less as needed. Refrigerate the shrimp until cooking time.

Heat the oil in a wok or frying pan. Usually 1/4 cup of oil is enough. This recipe will work well in a nonstick pan. Gently fry the shrimp until golden brown on both sides. Drain on paper towels. Serve at once, with the bowls of ketchup and mustard. This will make two generous portions.

Uncle Biddle's Baked Lobster

3 lobsters, 2–3 lb each, split in half
2 cups crumbled white bread
salt and pepper to taste
1/2 cup butter
parsley and lemon wedges

The California lobster is a different variety from those on the East Coast. It does not have those large claws that are a bit of a mess to crack and eat; instead, its entire body is completely filled with delicate lobster meat.

My Uncle Biddle was always my favorite. He drove an old Cadillac between his little ranch in Ensenada and my grandmother's apartment in Hermosa Beach. Uncle Biddle and Aunt Ruth always craved lobster when they arrived in Hermosa. I would go with them to the Redondo pier where he would pick the most peppy live lobsters from the salt water tank. The market would split them in half for him.

The lobsters were spread out on a baking sheet in my grandmother's kitchen while my uncle prepared a little "stuffing" for the small cavity between the meat and shell. His lobster philosophy was that if a lobster was baked instead of broiled it would cook evenly from top to bottom. He would never think of buying an already prepared boiled lobster.

My grandmother, aunt, and uncle would sip sherry while they waited for the lobsters to cook. Usually we had some fluffy hot mashed potatoes and a romaine lettuce salad with the lobster. California lobsters prepared this way are a terrific treat.

When you arrive home from the fish market, gently rinse out the lobsters, removing any undesired insides. Store in the refrigerator, cut side down for drainage, until ready to cook.

Melt 4 T. of the butter in a little frying pan. Lightly brown the bread with salt and pepper with a little minced parsley. Use this to fill the little cavity by the lobster's head. Dab lobsters with remaining butter, and salt and pepper to taste. Bake at 350° for 30–40 minutes until cooked. The shells will be red and the meat hot and white. Garnish with parsley and some lemon wedges. This will serve 3.

Bay Sand Dabs Meunière

Sand dabs are small delicate fish that seem to be on every menu in San Francisco. In traditional restaurants, the fish is presented on a heated white plate with the classic garnishes of parsley, lemon wedges, and maybe a simple boiled potato. In trendy spots, the fish may be served on a bed of basmati rice with diced red and green chilies, or perhaps various mashed potato concoctions with baby vegetables.

Timing is important in cooking these fragile fish. They must be treated gently; if cooked too long they will fall apart.

Place the flour on waxed paper or a plate. Carefully pat each piece of fish into the flour on both sides, adding more flour if needed. Meunière means "the miller's wife"; and you know she was not skimpy with flour.

Warm 1/4 cup of butter in a heavy frying pan until foamy and light brown. Cook the fish

1 lb sand dabs (skinned), sole may also be used
1/4 cup flour
1/2 cup butter plus an additional 1/4 cup
salt and pepper to taste
1 tsp. minced parsley
juice of one medium sized fresh lemon
parsley and lemon wedges for garnish

in the butter until golden brown, turning so both sides are done. Season with salt and pepper. You will very likely have to do this cooking in batches, adding an additional 1/4 cup of butter as you cook. Remove the fish to a warm platter.

Remove the frying butter from the pan, and wipe the pan clean with a paper towel. Add remaining 1/4 cup butter. Heat to melt, then add lemon juice and parsley. Pour over the fish. Serve at once with the lemon wedges and a few parsley leaves around the edge of the platter. This will serve 4 with light appetites, or 2 who are hungrier.

Party Fish Kebabs

Outdoor entertaining is a way of life in California, where the slightest excuse can be a reason for an outside party. It might be just to celebrate a beautiful spring day, out-of-town friends, birthdays, or any happy event.

Fish kebabs are a perfect choice for this kind of impromptu occasion. They are at their best cooked on a barbecue; however, if the day should turn coolish they can be cooked on an inside stove broiler. Rice, fresh seasonal vegetables, and green salad will complete the party meal. Chilled chardonnay or Sauvignon Blanc go well with these kebabs.

Cut the fish into one-inch cubes. Combine remaining ingredients (except bay), blending with a fork in a bowl. Place the fish in this marinade and refrigerate for 2–3 hours.

2 lb fresh swordfish or shark

1-1/4 cup olive oil

juice from one medium lemon

1/4 cup dry white wine

1/2 tsp. paprika

2 T. onion juice (simply run a raw onion over a grater)

salt and pepper to taste

20 bay leaves (fresh preferred)

To prepare for the barbecue, remove the fish from the marinade. Thread on metal skewers, placing an occasional bay leaf between the fish cubes. Barbecue or broil, keeping the fish around 5 inches from the fire. Baste with the marinade while turning the skewers so the fish is lightly browned on both sides. Serve by sliding fish off skewer onto a bed of rice. This will serve 4, but the recipe can be easily increased for larger parties.

Garlic and Lemon Flavored Shrimp

Everyone loves shrimp, especially in California, where the supermarkets are full of all sizes and types of shrimp: cooked, raw, shell on, shell off, baby, and jumbo. This recipe is one of the easiest ways to prepare shrimp. They will come out looking lovely, and be full of a marvelous zesty lemon and garlic flavor.

In a frying pan (a nonstick pan will work well) melt the butter, add the oil, and heat to medium-hot. Place some flour on a piece of waxed paper. Gently coat the shrimp with the flour—just a light coating. Place in the pan, adding the garlic at the same time. Stir fry until the shrimp is cooked (they will be pink and hot—do not overcook). Season with salt and pepper, add the lemon juice, and stir briefly. Serve at once with the lemony pan juices. This will serve 2–3.

1 lb large shrimp, peeled and deveined
1/2 cup flour
3 T. butter
2 T. olive oil
3 cloves garlic, peeled and minced
juice of one medium lemon
salt and pepper to taste

Baked Red Snapper in an Orange Citrus Sauce

1 lb red snapper filets
1/4 cup fresh orange juice
1 tsp. grated orange rind
1 T. soy sauce
1 T. sesame oil
2 T. minced green onion tops
salt and pepper to taste

Baking is a simple and healthy way of cooking fish. This recipe combines orange flavors with the popular Pacific trend of soy and sesame to make a delightful dinner. Serve with hot steamed rice and sliced cucumbers.

Combine all ingredients (except fish) in a shallow baking dish, large enough to fit the fish in one single layer. Stir with fork to blend ingredients. Add the fish and cover with the marinade. Refrigerate at least one hour to absorb flavors.

Heat oven to 400°. Place the pan in the oven, uncovered, and bake for 10 minutes or until the fish is cooked. Baste once with the sauce while cooking. Be careful not to overcook. To serve, place the fish with sauce on warmed plates. You might like to add a few orange slices for a garnish. This will serve 2. The fish may also be served chilled for hot weather dining.

Abalone Dreams

I do dream of abalone, because it has become very rare in California. Abalone is a single-shelled mollusk that clings to rocks in the ocean, at depths ranging from a few feet to over 100 feet. They were part of the diet of coastal Indians, who crafted the shells into jewelry and even fish hooks. We do not know how the Indians prepared their abalone, but an archaeologist's guess is that maybe it was eaten raw. The Indians did not leave any cookbooks behind.

The muscle that is the edible part must first be removed from the shell. It is then sliced thin and gently pounded. Abalone is slippery and it is a bit of a trick to slice and tenderize it. My son designed a special pounder for this task. We gave one to Julia Child, who named it "The Whackerspoon." I have pounded a lot of abalone in my kitchen and days later have discovered little flecks clinging to ceiling and walls. Sadly, these days are

> *2 abalone (8–9 inches across)*
> *2 eggs, beaten*
> *1 cup or more cracker meal*
> *salt and pepper to taste*
> *1/4 lb butter*
> *parsley and lemon wedges for garnish*

past, as my husband and son and other diving friends are no longer able to find any abalone. Pollution, sea otters, and disease have taken their toll.

The progress being made in abalone farming offers a ray of hope for the future. A very few restaurants and some special fish markets offer abalone, but due to scarcity, it is expensive. It is a most unique sea taste, unlike any other sea creature and worth every cent. If you should be lucky enough to have some to cook at home, this is how it is done.

Slice the abalone transversely into "steaks" about half an inch thick. Lay them on a wooden board and pound with a meat pounder until the abalone feels tender and relaxed. Dip the steaks into the cracker meal and then into the eggs.

Melt half of the butter in a frying pan. Heavy iron pans work the best. Fry the abalone on each side until light brown. Season with salt and pepper. They only take a minute or so on each side—overcooking makes them tough. You will have to do this in batches, so add the remaining butter as needed. Season with salt and pepper and serve on warmed plates garnished with parsley and lemon. This will serve 2–3.

Trout with Mushrooms

4 fresh or frozen trout (3–4 lb)
1/2 cup butter (1 4-oz. cube)
1/4 cup vegetable or peanut oil
flour for dusting
salt and pepper to taste
1/2 lb fresh mushrooms
lemon wedges and parsley for garnishing

California is full of rushing and gurgling streams and trout flourish here. They are very quick and it takes cunning and experience to catch these shimmering fish.

The many fish farms up and down the state make it possible to serve trout even if you are not an expert fisherman. Supermarket fish sections carry farm-raised trout that are delicate and delicious.

Pat the trout dry with paper towels. Dust with flour, and sprinkle with salt and pepper to your taste. Heat 1/2 of the butter with oil in a large frying pan. When well heated, place the trout in the pan. Brown on both sides. This will take about 5 minute for each side.

Wash and dry the mushrooms, and slice them thinly. Heat the remaining butter in a small frying pan. Gently fry the mushrooms over a low flame for a few minutes. Season with salt and pepper. Remove from the heat.

Place the trout on a warmed serving platter. Scatter the mushrooms over the trout, then garnish with lemon and parsley. Traditionally this is served with plain boiled potatoes. This will serve 4.

Sole Veronique

Veronique was a comic opera written by the Frenchman, Andre Messager. August Escoffier, the master chef, created this special recipe in 1903 to celebrate the French troupe's performance. Since that time this lovely recipe has become popular worldwide. Its use of wine and grapes has made it a natural favorite in California.

1 lb filet of sole slices
flour for dusting
salt and pepper to taste
2 T. vegetable or peanut oil
3 T. butter
1/2 cup white wine
32 (about) white seedless grapes,
   peeled or unpeeled

Dust the sole with flour. Heat the butter in a frying pan. Gently cook each filet on both sides until golden brown. Season with salt and pepper. This may have to be done in two batches, and you may need additional butter or oil for the frying.

When the sole is cooked, remove to a warm platter. Add the wine and grapes to the butter in the pan, stirring till the grapes are just barely warmed. I prefer to peel the grapes first, if I have the time. Peeling grapes is relaxing and adds class to this recipe.

Pour the sauce over the cooked sole. If you have fresh grape leaves, or little bunches of grapes, they make a pretty garnish on the platter. This will serve 3.

Oyster Peace Loaf

California men like to socialize, as do men everywhere. In the early days of San Francisco there was much to discuss: the latest news from the gold fields, real estate prices, government, the legality of land grants, and the current entertainment in the city. It became a tradition to take a "peace" offering to the lady waiting at home, to make up for returning at a late hour. Several establishments specialized in this unique loaf. The Chinese cook at Gobey's Oyster Palace was famous for his. He used Eastern oysters and would wrap the loaf carefully in brown paper so it would arrive toasty hot. This makes a very tasty late night snack, especially when served with a bottle of champagne.

Dip the oysters in the egg, then roll in the meal or crumbs. Heat the oil and one half of the butter cube in a frying pan. Fry the oysters until golden brown on each side, seasoning with salt and pepper.

Cut the loaf of bread lengthwise, making the bottom half larger than the top. The idea is to make a sort of bread "basket." The top is the

1 long loaf of French bread

12 medium sized oysters, drained

1 egg, slightly beaten

*cracker meal or fine bread crumbs
as needed*

1/4 cup peanut or vegetable oil

1/2 cup butter (4 oz.)

salt and pepper to taste

lid. Remove some of the bread from the inside of the bottom half. This is where the oysters will be placed. Spread remaining butter over the inside top and bottom of the bread. Additional butter may be used if desired.

Place the bread in a 300° oven for 5–8 minutes. It should be crusty and slightly warm. Fill the bottom half with the fried oysters. Put the lid on, and press together gently. If you are planning to use this for a picnic, wrap in a clean dish towel for transporting to the site. Oyster loaf can also be made using individual French rolls. How many this will serve depends on oyster loaf appetites. There are some who can easily devour the entire loaf.

Wharf Deviled Crab

San Francisco is a city of crab fans, and its old cookbooks are filled with crab recipes. All the tourist restaurants on the wharf and city dining spots offer many variations on crab dishes. One of the oldest and most popular is this easy version of deviled crab.

Melt the butter in a heavy saucepan. Add bell pepper and onion, and sauté over a low flame just until limp. Add flour to pan and blend.

Slowly add the half-and-half, cayenne, and mustard. Stir until the mixture is slightly thick. Add the brandy and crab.

Place in a buttered baking dish, or 4 individual baking dishes or shells. Sprinkle bread crumbs on top. Bake at 350° for 20 minutes. Garnish with a little minced parsley and serve to 4.

1/4 cup butter

1 green or red bell pepper, seeded and diced in small pieces

4 green onions, minced

1 T. flour

2 cups half-and-half (or cream)

1/4 tsp. cayenne pepper

2 T. Dijon mustard

salt to taste

2 T. brandy

1 lb crab meat

1/4 cup bread crumbs

minced parsley for garnish

Spring Salmon with Cucumber Garnish

A springtime drive through any of California's vineyards is an exhilarating experience. The tender new grape buds are pale green with a pinkish tinge, a beautiful promise of the summer's grape harvest. Delicate pink salmon combined with pale green cucumber is a perfect dinner for this lovely season.

Melt the butter. Mix with the lemon juice, salt, pepper, and white wine. Place the salmon in a shallow baking dish that will fit the fish pieces, and pour the seasoned liquid over it. Cover with foil. Bake at 350° for 25 minutes, or until salmon is cooked. It will be pink and flake easily.

While the salmon is cooking, peel the cucumber and remove the seeds. Dice into

> 4 serving pieces of salmon (either filets or steaks; about 3 to 3-1/2 lb)
> 1/4 cup butter
> juice of one medium lemon
> salt and pepper to taste
> 1/4 cup dry white wine
> 1 cucumber
> minced parsley

quarter-inch cubes. Cook the cubes 5 minutes in simmering water. Drain immediately and set aside.

To serve, place each salmon steak on a warmed plate. Pour the juices from the pan over the salmon servings. Strew with cucumber and garnish with some finely minced parsley. Boiled new butter potatoes are a good accompaniment for this main dish.

Poultry

Golden State Variations

In Southern California some years ago, the ideal Sunday entertainment was to drive to Knott's Berry Farm and enjoy a dinner of fried chicken served with fresh biscuits and a side dish of rhubarb. Dessert was berry pie. Chicken on Sunday seemed to be in tune with the Roosevelt philosophy that every American was entitled to a chicken in the pot. Henri IV of France had also had this dream, hoping to make France so prosperous that every peasant would have a chicken in his pot on Sunday.

This trend of thought continues today, as Californians devour more chicken than any other food. It may be grilled on an outdoor barbecue, served in an oriental stir-fry, or Mexican style in tortillas. Chicken may conveniently be bought whole, cut up, skinned, or filleted at very competitive prices. This chapter contains both classic and trendier new recipes to try with this endlessly popular, versatile bird.

North Beach Chicken Cacciatora

1 3–4 lb chicken, cut up, or chicken
  parts
1/2 cup flour
1/4 cup olive oil
1 medium sized onion, chopped
2 cloves fresh garlic, minced
1/4 cup red or white wine vinegar
1/2 tsp. dried or fresh thyme
1/2 tsp. dried or fresh oregano
salt and pepper to taste
2 cups canned whole tomatoes
1 chopped red or green bell pepper
1 cup sliced fresh mushrooms
1/4 cup chopped olives
1/4 cup white wine

The Italians who settled in San Francisco's North Beach section brought their recipes from home. Some families opened restaurants, many of which still survive today. Strolling around this area is one of the many special things to do while visiting San Francisco. You will hear Italian spoken on the streets and find an exciting selection of food stores and shops. Finish your walk with a lunch or dinner in any of the classical Italian restaurants in the neighborhood.

Chicken Cacciatora is one of the timeless old world Italian recipes.

The first step is to coat the chicken with flour. The simplest way to do this is by the old-fashioned method of placing the flour in a paper bag, adding the chicken, and shaking to coat it with flour.

Heat the oil in a large frying pan and brown the chicken on both sides. This may have to be done in two batches. Remove the chicken, and add onion and garlic to the same pan. Fry just until limp, then stir in the wine vinegar and seasonings. Add the tomatoes, breaking up any large pieces. Next, add the bell pepper, mushrooms, olives, wine, and chicken. Cover and simmer until chicken is tender—about 45 minutes. This dish may also be baked in a 350° oven for 45 minutes. This will serve 4–5. Be sure to serve some good Italian bread to dunk in the flavorful juices.

Gala Chicken Curry

Curry dinners are popular for California parties. Pretty dishes filled with condiments are placed on a buffet table to accompany the curry. Guests help themselves from this colorful assortment of chopped peanuts, minced green onions, crumbled cooked bacon, chopped hard boiled egg, chutney, and grated coconut.

Fresh tropical fruits (pineapple, papaya, mango, melon) are often sliced and served as side dishes with curries.

Heat the oil or butter in a large pot. Peel and core the apples, then chop with the green pepper and onions. Stir around in the pot, cooking just until limp. Mix in the flour and curry powder, stirring to blend. Add salt, stock, wine, and lemon. Simmer uncovered for 15 minutes on a low flame. Add chicken and simmer another 15 minutes. This will serve 4. A pot of hot steamed rice is usually served as an accompaniment.

2 T. olive oil or butter
2 cooking apples
1 green pepper, seeded
2 onions
2 T. flour
1 T. curry powder
1/2 tsp. salt
1-1/2 cups chicken stock
1/2 cup white wine
1 lemon, juice and grated rind
2 cups cooked cubed chicken

Chicken Divan

Chicken Divan is a nostalgic recipe from the twenties. It originated in New York, swept the country, and was a favorite main dish in California for many years. Perhaps because of overexposure it sort of faded away. It deserves a revival because it is flavorful, attractive, and perfect for a little dinner party.

Cover the chicken breasts with lightly salted water. Simmer until tender, about 25 minutes. Cool in the liquid. Cut the breasts in long slices. Set aside. This may be done ahead.

Trim the broccoli so that you have nice bite-sized pieces. Steam or simmer just until tender. Drain, and place in a buttered oven-proof pan. Carefully lay the chicken slices on top.

Make the sauce by melting 3 T. of the butter in a saucepan. Add flour and stir. Gradually add the milk, stirring to avoid lumps. Cut the remaining 3 T. butter in tiny pieces and

3 boneless chicken breasts (about 3 to 3-1/2 lb)
1-1/2 lb fresh broccoli, or two 10-oz pkgs. frozen

Easy Hollandaise Sauce

6 T. butter
3 T. flour
1-1/2 cups milk
2 egg yolks, slightly beaten
3 T. fresh lemon juice
1/2 cup Parmesan cheese

add with the egg yolks to the milk. Continue stirring, adding lemon juice. The sauce should be smooth and slightly thick. Pour over the chicken, and sprinkle the top with Parmesan cheese. Place about 5 inches below a broiler on "low" temperature. Broil until the top is brown and the dish bubbly. This will take about 8 minutes. Turkey slices may be substituted for chicken. Serve with mashed potatoes or pasta. This will serve 4.

Chicken Breasts with Prosciutto and Cheese

If you are searching for the perfect dinner party entree, this combination will always be a winner. The flavors are Italian with a California touch. It can be prepared the day ahead and heated in the oven while your guests are nibbling antipasto and sipping wine.

Cut each breast in half so you have 8 pieces (this is already done in some supermarket packages). Place them between sheets of waxed paper and flatten with a meat pounder or the bottom of a heavy bottle. Sprinkle with salt and pepper. Dust with flour.

Heat the butter and oil in a frying pan. Lightly brown the chicken on each side. This will only take a few minutes. If chicken breasts without skin are overcooked, they become dry.

In a large baking pan, place a thin layer of olive oil. Place the chicken pieces in the pan. Lay a piece of prosciutto on each piece. Top

4 medium sized (3 to 3-1/2 lb) boneless, skinless chicken breasts

8 thin slices of prosciutto

1/4 lb fontina, Swiss, or Jack cheese, sliced thin

salt and pepper to taste

flour

3 T. olive oil, plus olive oil for baking pan

3 T. butter

1 T. sage (minced if fresh; crushed if dried)

Parmesan cheese

1/2 cup white wine

with a cheese slice. Sprinkle sage over all. Dribble the wine over chicken. Sprinkle with Parmesan cheese. Cover with foil and bake in a 300° oven for 20 minutes. If you have made this dish ahead and it is cold, add 10 minutes more baking time. Serve with pasta, green salad, crusty bread, and a chilled chardonnay or Sauvignon Blanc. This will serve 4.

Viva la Chicken

Viva la Chicken is a mixture of chicken layered between tortilla strips, cheese, soups, and seasonings. It is made ahead and all the ingredients are refrigerated for 24 hours to mellow together in a delicious result. In California, it is used as a light dish for supper, lunch, or brunch. This is a handy recipe and always a favorite for a party.

Cut the chicken breasts in small chunks. In a large bowl mix the soups, milk, salsa, onion, chiles, and chicken.

Grease a large baking pan. In the bottom of the pan place the 3 T. of liquid. Layer half the tortilla strips in the pan. Place half of the chicken mixture on top of the tortillas. Add half the cheese. Place the remaining tortillas on top of chicken. Finish with the remaining chicken and then the remaining cheese. Cover with foil and refrigerate overnight or up to 24 hours.

3–4 lb cooked boneless chicken breasts

1 can cream of chicken soup (10-3/4 oz.)

1 can cream of mushroom soup (10-3/4 oz.)

1 cup milk or half-and-half

2 cups bottled Mexican salsa

1 onion, minced

1 can diced green chiles (4 oz.)

1 dozen corn tortillas, cut in 1 inch strips

3 T. liquid (chicken broth, water, or white wine)

1 lb cheddar or Jack cheese, grated

sliced olives and fresh cilantro for garnish

Bake at 300°, uncovered, for about an hour and 15 minutes. The top should be bubbly and light brown. Garnish with olives and cilantro. This will serve 10.

Chicken in a Red Wine Sauce

Wine makers in California like to cook chicken with their red wine. It is a sort of California version of the French coq au vin, as the chicken pieces are slowly baked in the red wine.

This is perfect for a party. Make it a day ahead so the lusty flavors will have time to mellow. Serve with mashed or boiled potatoes to soak up the delicious juices. A merlot or Burgundy is a good choice for both the cooking and drinking wine.

Pat the chicken dry and dredge in the flour. Heat the butter and oil in a large oven casserole. Add chicken pieces and lightly brown a few at a time, adding more butter or oil if necessary. Return all pieces to the pot. Add remaining ingredients except the wine and brandy.

Pour the brandy or cognac over the chicken and light with a match. Do not get your face

2 chickens, about 3 lb each, cut in serving pieces
flour for coating the chicken
6 T. butter
2 T. cooking oil
1/4 lb diced ham (or lean uncooked bacon, diced)
1/4 lb fresh mushrooms, sliced
18 small boiling onions, peeled
1 tsp. thyme, dried or fresh
salt and pepper to taste
1 bay leaf
1/4 cup brandy or cognac
4 cups dry red wine, plus more if needed

too close to the flame. When the flame dies out, add the wine. Stir and cover casserole. Bake in a 325° oven for an hour, or until chicken is tender. Stir now and then during the baking, adding more wine if necessary. This will serve 8.

69

Chicken Jerusalem

Chicken combined with artichoke hearts is a San Francisco classic. The name comes from the Jerusalem artichokes that were originally used in this recipe. Today artichoke hearts are used. Chicken Jerusalem is a good choice for a company dish. It is lovely and classy, and can all be made ahead so last-minute hustle and bustle are avoided.

Cut the chicken breasts into 1-1/2 inch squares or as close as is possible. Place the lemon juice in a bowl, add the chicken, stir to coat, and marinate 30 minutes.

Cook the artichokes as per package directions and drain. Place the drained artichokes in a lightly buttered casserole.

Remove the chicken from the lemon juice, shaking off excess juice. Dust with flour. Melt the butter in a frying pan, and brown the chicken lightly on both sides. Season with salt and pepper. Add the sherry, cover

2 boned and skinned chicken breasts (about 1-1/4 to 1-1/2 lb)

2 T. lemon juice

1 9-oz. pkg. frozen artichoke hearts, or 1 14-oz. can artichoke hearts. If using canned, drain and cut each piece in half.

flour for dusting chicken

1/2 cup butter (4 oz.)

salt and pepper to taste

1/3 cup dry sherry

Sauce

1 T. butter

1 T. flour

1 cup half-and-half

salt and pepper to taste

chives or parsley for garnish

the pan, and cook over a low flame for 10 minutes. Lay the chicken, with any pan juices, on top of the artichokes.

To make the sauce, melt the butter in a saucepan, add flour, and blend. Stir in half-and-half, salt, and pepper. Cook over low flame, stirring until the sauce is slightly thick. Pour over chicken. Bake, uncovered, at 350° for 20 minutes. If dish has been made ahead and refrigerated, add about 15 extra minutes for baking. This will serve 3 and may be doubled for a party. Garnish with minced parsley or chives. Hot mashed potatoes or steamed rice go very well with Chicken Jerusalem.

J and J Tasty Chicken Wings

J and J is not some mysterious ingredient. The initials stand for my friends Joanne and Judy. We have all been docents at the Los Angeles Museum of Natural History. Joanne and Judy created this easy dish for potlucks, training classes, field trips, and birthdays. The wings are marinated, cooked, and served all from the same pot. It is easy and always popular. It may be served hot or cold; if serving cold remove any bits of accumulated fat from the top (it looks ugly).

Cut each chicken wing at the joint to make two pieces. Cut off and discard the tips.

Combine remaining ingredients and heat in a saucepan until the butter is melted. Stir and remove from flame. Arrange the chicken

4 lb chicken wings
1 cup soy sauce
1 cup brown sugar
1/4 cup butter
1 T. fresh grated ginger (optional)
1 tsp. hot or Dijon-style mustard
3/4 cup water
*lime slices, fresh cilantro, or diced
   pineapple for garnish*

wings in a shallow baking pan. When the sauce is cool, pour over the wings and mix for even coating. Refrigerate and marinate overnight, or at least four hours. Give the wings a stir during the marinating for better flavor absorption.

Bake at 350° for 45 minutes, stirring now and then. Drain and serve either hot or cold, with desired garnishes.

San Francisco Canton Chop Suey

It may seem curious that Canton chop suey is not really a Cantonese creation. The dish originated in San Francisco with a Chinese chef, who created it for a banquet in honor of Li Hung Chang, the first Chinese viceroy to visit San Francisco. In Cantonese, the words mean "odds and ends." For the home cook, chop suey is an easy and tasty way to use leftover chicken (pork may also be used). This recipe can be varied and always makes a most appetizing meal.

Cut the meat in julienne strips about 1/4 inch wide and 2 inches long. Slice the onions and celery diagonally.

Heat the oil in a wok or large frying pan. Add the meat, onions, celery, peppers, and

2 cups cooked chicken (or pork)
4 whole green onions
1/2 cup celery
1 green pepper, diced
1 cup fresh sliced mushrooms
1 cup bean sprouts
3 T. peanut or other cooking oil
1 tsp. cornstarch
2 T. soy sauce
1 cup chicken broth

mushrooms. Stir fry for 5 minutes, then add the bean sprouts. In a bowl, mix the cornstarch and soy sauce with the chicken broth. Add to pan mixture. Stir until the liquid is slightly thickened. Serve with hot rice. This will feed 4.

King Tut Chicken Kebabs

Californians have often been swept away by things. There are Egyptian theaters, museums, restaurants, and street names. The ruins of Egyptian temples built for the movie *Cleopatra* lie buried in the shifting sands near Nipomo. When the treasures from King Tut's tomb were displayed at the Los Angeles County Museum, the lines were blocks long. There was a sort of Tutmania in Los Angeles. As many restaurants were featuring Egyptian cuisine, I decided to do a series of cooking classes from this mystic country. Among the most popular recipes were these sort of exotic kebabs.

Cut each chicken breast into small bite-sized pieces. Combine the yogurt, curry, lemon juice, and salt. Mix, and marinate the chicken in this mixture for one hour or longer.

2 whole chicken breasts, skinned and boned
1 cup plain yogurt
1/4 tsp. salt
2 tsp. curry powder
1 tsp. lemon juice
8 thin slices white onion (or 8 small boiling onions)
8 cherry tomatoes, halved

Thread on skewers, with onions and tomatoes in between every two or so chicken pieces. Broil over charcoal or in your oven broiler, turning until chicken is cooked (about 10 minutes) and basting with marinade. Garnish with melon slices or grapes. This will serve 4.

Fiesta Chicken Enchiladas

Fiestas are part of the California heritage. During the days of the great Spanish ranches, fiestas would be held to celebrate weddings, births, roundups, harvests, or for just any excuse. The early Californians loved to party and dance. The mission cuisine brought the Mexican tradition of making tortillas. They were made with flour, as wheat was easily grown in the mission fields.

Barbecued meats were main dishes at fiestas, served with huge trays of enchiladas. The guests partied and feasted far into the night. Celebrations lasted several days and guests always were given overnight accommodations. This modern recipe has its beginnings in the rancho heritage.

Bone, skin, and then shred chicken breasts in long pieces. Cream the cheese with a wooden spoon until smooth. Mix in the chicken, green onions, salt and pepper, and one half of the diced chiles. Now mix in one

12 medium size flour or corn tortillas

2 whole cooked chicken breasts

1 8-oz. pkg. cream cheese (room temperature)

6 green onions, minced

salt and pepper to taste

1 4-oz. can diced green chiles

2 cups grated Jack cheese

1 cup sour cream

1 8-oz. can tomato sauce

1 tsp. chili powder

oil for frying, if corn tortillas are used

cilantro, avocado slices for garnish (optional)

cup of the Jack cheese. This is the filling, and it can be prepared ahead.

If flour tortillas are used, simply heat until limp on a frying pan or griddle. If you use corn tortillas, heat a little oil in a frying pan and fry each tortilla until limp, adding oil as needed. Drain on paper towels.

(continued on next page)

(continued from previous page)

Fill each tortilla with about 2 T. of the filling. Roll the tortilla and place seam side down in a lightly greased baking pan.

Mix the sour cream with the tomato sauce, chili powder and remaining diced chiles. Spoon over tortillas. Sprinkle with remaining cheese and bake, uncovered, for 20 minutes at 325°. They should just be hot, with the cheese melted. You do not want the enchiladas to get mushy. Garnish as desired. I like pale green avocado slices arranged on the top. This will serve 6.

Nana's Southern Gumbo

"Nana," my grandmother on my mother's side, was from Myrtle Grove, Louisiana. She loved to tell stories about plantation life. She told how they made gumbo: early every morning, shrimp peddlers would arrive, hawking incredibly fresh gulf shrimp. The family's cook would pick out the finest shrimp. Fresh chickens from the poultry yard would be prepared, along with ham from the smoke house. Okra grew in the garden. These ingredients were all combined with seasonings, and cooked and served with large bowls of rice.

In Nana's youth she fell passionately in love with a dashing Spanish man. Her parents did not approve of Fernando and sent her off to New York to a finishing school and further education, including piano lessons. As luck would have it, my future grandfather was her piano teacher. They fell in love and were married Christmas Eve in New York's Riverside Church during a light snowfall.

1/4 cup vegetable or peanut oil to fry the chicken

1 whole chicken (about 3 lb), cut up

1 cup diced ham

1 large onion, chopped

salt and pepper to taste

2 T. parsley

1 28-oz. can solid pack tomatoes

3 cups of okra, sliced (fresh, frozen, or canned)

1 lb medium shrimp, peeled and deveined

Nana did not like living in New York. My grandfather's brother urged him to come to Pasadena and start a music school. Of course, Nana said yes, and they came to California with their four children.

Summer is hot in Pasadena, and it was the family custom to spend the season in Hermosa Beach, enjoying the ocean breezes. When my grandfather retired they decided to live in Hermosa Beach all the year. Their apartment had an ocean view and room for a

(continued on next page)

(continued from previous page)

piano. The kitchen was large and cheery with a breakfast nook. This is where I learned to make gumbo and cook with both of them. Gumbo is a terrific party dish. Try and allow enough time to prepare it ahead so the flavors can have a day to mellow.

In a large frying pan, fry the chicken pieces, ham, and onion until lightly browned. This procedure is sort of a light stir-fry to give a browned flavor and seal in the chicken juices. Remove to a large soup pot or preferably an iron Dutch oven. Add salt, pepper, parsley, and tomatoes. Cut up any large pieces of tomato. You may add a half cup of white wine, if desired. The liquid should just cover the chicken; if it is low, add stock or water. Cover and simmer until the chicken is tender, about 45 minutes. Remove chicken, and when it is cool enough to handle, remove the meat from the bones. Return the meat to the pot and cook with okra, uncovered, for an additional 10 minutes, adding the seafood for the last 7 minutes. Nana and my mother did not use filé powder, as they felt the okra provided enough thickening. This will serve 6. With the recent popularity of Louisiana sausages, some cooks today replace ham with sausage slices. Rice is always served with gumbo.

Szechwan Kung Pao Chicken

Chinese cooking has always appealed to Californians, and you will find a Chinese restaurant in almost every town. In the last two decades, more Californians have been able to travel to China and come home with recipes and cravings for Chinese food.

The Chinese province of Szechwan is in the upper basin of the Yangtze River. It has hot steamy summers, cold winters, and a hot peppery cuisine. This style of cooking, and this particular spicy dish, have become especially popular in California.

Cut the chicken into 3/4-inch squares. Combine remaining ingredients and stir well. Marinate the chicken cubes in this mixture overnight or at least for one hour.

In a wok or frying pan, heat 1/4 cup of peanut oil and stir fry the chicken cubes until just done—do not overcook. Remove the chicken. If necessary, add a little more

Chicken and Marinade

2 whole boneless chicken breasts
(1 to 1-1/2 lb)

1 tsp. salt and 1/2 tsp. white pepper

1 tsp. sesame oil

1 T. cornstarch

1 T. sherry or white wine

In a bowl combine the following:

The Bowl Ingredients

1 green pepper, slivered

1/2 cup water chestnuts, sliced

2 whole green onions, thinly sliced

8–10 mushrooms, sliced

1 clove of garlic, minced

1 T. fresh ginger, minced

Additional Ingredients

1/4 to 1/2 cup peanut oil

2–3 hot dried red peppers

3/4 cup chicken broth

1 T. soy sauce

1 T. cornstarch

1/2 cup toasted walnuts, or peanuts

oil. Stir fry the bowl ingredients for a few minutes.

Now, for the Szechwan touch, take 2–3 red peppers and snip into tiny pieces. The seeds may be discarded if you want a less hot flavor. Add these to the pot. Return the chicken. Mix the broth with soy and cornstarch. Add to the pan and stir all together until the sauce is thick. It will only take a minute or so. Add nuts and give another stir. Serve at once to 4, with boiled rice.

Sicilian Lemon Chicken

Sicily and California have some things in common, among them a warm climate, lemon groves, and a cuisine that uses the lemons. Sicilians love to cook with lemons, as do Californians. This tangy lemon-flavored chicken can be served hot, or chilled for picnics.

Combine the olive oil, lemon juice, garlic, and oregano. Place the chicken in a bowl and pour this marinade over it. Stir so chicken is covered on all sides. Marinate in the refrigerator several hours or overnight. Turn the pieces around once or twice for better absorption of flavor.

1 3–4 lb chicken, cut up (or your favorite parts)
1/4 cup olive oil
juice from 1 medium sized lemon, about 1/4 cup
2 cloves of fresh garlic, minced
1 T. oregano, fresh or dried
salt and pepper to taste
lemon wedges for garnish

Place in a flat baking pan. Cover with marinade. Sprinkle with salt and pepper. Bake uncovered at 350° for 1 hour, turning the pieces around several times. Serve garnished with lemon wedges. This will serve 6.

Meats

Beef, Pork, and Lamb

Cattle were brought to California by the explorer Juan Bautista de Anza. He delivered a small herd of cattle to the San Gabriel Mission, where they thrived and fed the Spanish garrisons, mission fathers, and their Indian converts. By the year 1834, the mission herds were said to number 400,000.

When Mexico seized California from Spain, the herds continued to increase. The cattle were raised for hides and tallow. Hides became the California bank note and were valued at two dollars each. The gold rush in 1849 created a huge demand for beef to feed the miners, and beef cattle were sold as high as $500 a head.

Beef was thus established in the California cuisine. In early ranch and pioneer days, the meat was roasted over open fires. Tougher cuts were made into stews, or dried and made into a kind of jerky (there was not any reliable refrigeration). Today, California cattlemen pride themselves on the high quality of California beef, and their ranches add beauty to the California landscape.

In the inland valleys, sheep were raised. Even today you will find Basque restaurants on the fringes of sheep herding land. The customers sit at long tables and are served the menu of the day, which consists of many filling courses and usually includes lamb. The Basques have been prominent in the state's sheep industry.

Pork is part of both Spanish and Mexican cuisine. The rancheros always had pigs in the barnyard. The ladies made chorizo, a spicy sausage, which was used to flavor beans and stews. Whole pigs were cooked in open pit barbecues for fiestas. Pork skin was made into chicharrones, or cracklings, still a favorite snack of the Mexican communities.

My personal nostalgic memories of meats include the prime ribs cooked for Christmas dinners. My mother would order the roast from her favorite butcher. When we opened the pink-wrapped package at home, the roast was carefully and neatly tied at perfectly spaced intervals with cute little knots. The roast was placed in the oven, rubbed with olive oil, and studded with inserts of fresh garlic. My mother would open the oven door to check on the cooking progress and delicious smells would fill the kitchen. When it was finally brought to the table there would be a discussion of which male would do the carving. The honor usually went to my Uncle Biddle, who had a way with a carving knife. My daddy would make sure that the young people and my grandmother always had a spoonful of the beef juice that collected at the bottom of the platter. This juice was considered extremely nourishing.

Roast pork with applesauce and mashed potatoes was certainly my absolute favorite childhood dinner. I went to Girl Scout camp in the San Bernardino mountains each summer. My parents would write and ask what I wanted for dinner when I came home, after basic camp food. They really knew, but liked to have fun with a little teasing. I would think about the pork and applesauce feast waiting for me all the way on the bus ride home. It always tasted fantastic.

Barbecue is a way of life in California. In the days preceding World War II, it was at a special culinary height. Custom barbecues were built for back yards by special barbecue contractors. Neighbors competed to have the latest style. Men did all the cooking. My father wore a chef's hat and a big apron with emblazoned words across the front saying "Barbecue Chef." Usually the menu was steaks with potatoes wrapped in foil tucked in the coals. Our custom barbecue even had a little oven incorporated in its design where plates and bread could stay warm. Barbecue evenings were very much a neighborhood affair. We would all take turns at entertaining. My neighborhood friends and I would run up and down the street bringing extra plates or food from one house to the next, having such fun.

Individual portions of meat may be smaller now than in the rancho days of the state, but barbecue remains a most popular way of preparing any meat. Ethnic influences have brought stir-fries and other current creative ways of using meat. Today, meat continues to be an important part of the state's cuisine.

Bride's Beef Burgundy

One thing I learned in my early married days was that it is very convenient, when entertaining, to prepare as much of the meal as possible ahead of time. Most of my cooking students worry about how to get everything to the table at the same time. This is a common problem. The easiest solution is to serve a one-pot main dish that can be made ahead of time, with a simple accompaniment.

Beef burgundy is perfect for company dinners, and actually improves by mellowing for a day. I like to serve it with steamed rice, a green salad, and crusty French bread on a cold foggy night.

Heat the oil or drippings in a heavy stew pot, and cook the onions just until limp. Remove with a slotted spoon and set aside. Lightly brown the beef cubes in the same oil, adding a little more if needed. When the meat is browned, stir in the flour and blend. Add the liquid and wine. Season with thyme, salt and

2 lb round, chuck, or stewing beef, cut in 1-1/2 inch cubes

3 T. vegetable oil (or bacon drippings)

4 medium white onions, peeled and sliced

2 T. flour

1 T. fresh or dried thyme

2 cups Burgundy or other dry red wine

1-1/2 cups beef stock, canned beef bouillon, or water

salt and pepper to taste

1/2 lb fresh mushrooms, sliced

parsley for garnish

pepper. Cover and bake at 325° for about two hours, until meat is tender. Stir now and then, adding additional wine if liquid is low. This may also be simmered on top of the stove.

Add the mushrooms for the last 30 minutes of cooking. Cool and refrigerate overnight, or for up to two days. This will serve 4. A bottle of California Burgundy will add the finishing touch to this easy, lusty, and delicious party dish.

Firehouse Chili

Brave firemen are part of California's past and present. In the early days of San Francisco, each household was required to always have six buckets of water on hand. When volunteer firemen were organized, fire fighting methods improved. These men were the heroes of the city. They were included in balls, parades, and civic events. It was a mark of distinction to be a fireman. There was a competitive spirit among the companies. Citizens would have their favorite brigades and run along with them to the fires to give their support.

One of the favorite tales of San Francisco's firemen is the rescue of Lillie Hitchcock when she was only nine years old. From that time on, firemen were her passion in life. She rode in their trucks, partied, danced and drank, and was their mascot. In her will, she left one hundred thousand dollars for a memorial, and fifty thousand dollars for a sculpture. The monument is Coit Tower, which is shaped like a fire nozzle, and the sculpture of a brave fireman stands in Washington Square.

2–3 T. oil or lard

1 onion, chopped

1 clove garlic, minced

1 jalapeño pepper, finely chopped (optional)

2 lb beef (boneless chuck or round steak) cut in 1/2-inch cubes

2 T. chili powder

salt and pepper to taste

1 T. ground cumin

1 cup liquid (beer, red wine, tequila, broth, etc.)

1 28-oz. can diced or crushed tomatoes

1 4-oz. can diced green chiles

Firemen have a reputation for good cooking. They have published their own cookbooks and are interviewed in cooking magazines. Chili is popular in the fire houses as it can be left waiting in the pot when the fire calls come ringing in.

I have often been a chili judge, sampling as many as twenty chili versions at one time. Beer is sipped between bites. In chili contest cooking, beans are not used, as it is felt they detract from authentic chili. If you like beans, of course, you can use them. Chili is a great party dish, when made ahead so the flavors can mellow and served with pretty bowls of toppings.

Heat the oil or lard in a stew pot. Lightly brown the onion, garlic and jalapeño pepper. Remove from the pot with a slotted spoon and set aside. Put the meat, chili powder and cumin into the pot and brown lightly, adding more oil if necessary. Return onions, garlic and pepper to the pot, along with liquid, tomatoes and green chiles. Cover and cook over a low flame for 1 hour and 15 minutes or until the meat is tender. Stir now and then during the cooking period. Serve in bowls to 4.

Chili cooks differ in their choice of liquids and in fact are very creative with chili recipes. This recipe is only a guide; add your own touches.

Toppings for chili may be placed on the table to add extra flavors to your steaming bowl of chili. The favorites are grated cheddar cheese, minced onions, sour cream, finely chopped green chiles, and olives.

Russian Hill Beef Stroganoff

Russian Hill is one of the largest of San Francisco's 52 hills. The name originated because a Russian ship exploring the coast had the misfortune to have some sailors die during a voyage from Russia to San Francisco. They were buried on this hill.

Russian sailors were enchanted by this city overlooking the bay. They left their ships and started a little Russian colony. Today, the Russian population in San Francisco is one of the largest in the country and a very important part of the cultural life of the city. Beef Stroganoff is a Russian-inspired dish that has always been a favorite for dinner parties in the bay city.

Remove any fat from the steak. Cut the meat into julienne strips about 2-1/2 inches long by 1/3 inch by 1/3 inch.

Divide butter in half. Place half the butter in a frying pan and melt over low flame. Add the onions and gently stir-fry until just limp.

1 lb filet mignon or top sirloin steak
1/4 cup butter
1 medium-sized white onion, thinly sliced
1/3 lb fresh mushrooms, thinly sliced
1/2 cup sour cream
salt and pepper to taste
Parsley for garnish

Do not let them brown. Add the sliced mushrooms. Stir with onions for a minute to cook.

In another frying pan, melt the remaining butter. Add the steak and stir-fry just until rare inside. Add the mushrooms and onions to the steak pan. Blend in the sour cream. Heat slightly, just until the cream is hot. Serve at once. The idea is that the steak should remain rare in the delectable mushroom-onion sauce. Garnish with parsley. This will serve 2. Usually this is served with rice or egg noodles. Chilled champagne will add a happy Russian mood.

Pepper Steak

Pepper steak been a popular main dish for many years. Sometimes if you are in a classy restaurant the waiter will carry the dramatically flaming platter to your table. This ritual is often part of a formal waiter's education. If you are cooking this steak at home and do not need to create a fiery impression, it is not necessary to do the flame procedure.

Pat the steaks dry with paper towels. Slash any fat along the edge of the steak at 2 inch intervals so the edges will not curl during cooking. Press the pepper into both sides of the steak, using 1 tsp. per steak. This may be done ahead, and the steaks refrigerated. If so, remove from refrigerator and let stand at room temperature for 20 minutes before cooking to help absorb pepper flavor.

In a heavy frying pan, heat the oil and butter over medium high heat. Fry steaks on each side until cooked to your preferred doneness. This will take about 4 minutes on each side for medium rare. Remove steaks to a

4 boneless steaks, about 3/4 lb each and 3/4 inch thick (New York or top sirloin)

4 tsp. coarsely ground pepper

3 T. butter

2 T. vegetable or peanut oil

1/4 cup brandy or cognac

1/2 cup dry white wine

2 T. cream plus an additional 1 T. butter

warm platter. Sometimes a light sprinkling of salt is added. Personally, I feel the pepper flavor is adequate.

Add the remaining 1 T. butter to the pan and swirl around. Next add the wine and cream to the pan. Cook briskly, scraping up the pan juices. When the sauce is slightly reduced, add the brandy or cognac. You may flame the liquor, or simply cook a few additional seconds. Pour over the steaks and serve to 4. Pepper steak has a French origin, and in that country the steaks are usually served with French fries and a few sprigs of fresh watercress.

Favorite Tamale Pie

Tamale pie has been used for entertaining in California for over a hundred years. Its flavors combine the state's Spanish and Mexican heritage. Tamale pie has remained popular because it is very tasty and easy to serve, and it can easily be prepared ahead to avoid last minute rushing in the kitchen. Serve it with a big green salad and hot tortillas.

Bring water to a boil in a large pot. Reduce heat to simmer. Slowly pour in the cornmeal, seasonings, and butter or oil. Stir with a wooden spoon to blend. Continue cooking over a low flame for 15 minutes, stirring now and then to prevent mixture from sticking to the bottom. Set aside.

In a large frying pan, heat the oil, then add meat and seasonings. Stir around to blend. Add onion and green pepper and continue to stir and fry until meat loses pink color. Next add tomatoes and corn. Some cooks like to add additional fresh chopped Anaheim chilies or canned diced green chilies. This is up to your taste. Simmer for 20 minutes, stirring now and then.

Cornmeal Crust

5 cups water

1 T. butter or olive oil

1 tsp. salt

1 tsp. chili powder

2-1/2 cups corn meal

Filling

1 T. vegetable oil or bacon drippings

1 medium onion, peeled and chopped

1 medium green or red bell pepper, chopped

1 lb ground beef

1 T. chili powder

1 tsp. cumin (optional)

salt to taste

1 28-oz. can diced or solid pack tomatoes (or 2 cups fresh, chopped)

1 cup fresh corn (scraped from cob) or 1 cup canned or frozen corn kernels

fresh chopped Anaheim chili, or canned green chili (optional)

Topping

1 cup grated cheddar cheese

1 cup pitted sliced black olives

To assemble, lightly grease a 2-quart (or close) shallow baking dish or casserole. Line with two thirds of the corn meal mixture. Add the filling, and top with remaining crust. You may have to dip your hands in cold water and sort of pat this topping around. Top with grated cheese and olives. Bake at 350° for 40 minutes. This will serve 6–8, depending on appetites.

Joan's Malaysia Satay

My special friend Joan and I have been friends since we were both pregnant many years ago. Now we are grandmothers, and have shared many happy times. Joan likes to collect recipes. One of her trips was to Malaysia, where she found this authentic street food recipe.

Satays are bite-sized pieces of meat, poultry, or fish, marinated in an exotic sauce and then broiled or barbecued. In Malaysia, vendors cook these satays on the street in little charcoal braziers. Satays have become very popular in California for appetizers or patio suppers.

1 lb boneless beef (flank or top sirloin). Pork, chicken, or firm fish may also be used.

1 T. sugar

4 entire green onions, chopped

2 T. curry powder

1 clove garlic, minced

Cut the meat into small bite-sized pieces. Combine remaining ingredients in a bowl. Add a little water and mix to make a paste. Marinate the meat in this mixture at least an hour or longer. Thread on skewers and broil or barbecue. Serve with the following sauce.

Malaysian Peanut Dunking Sauce

Chop peanuts very fine (you can use a blender or processor). Combine with the remaining ingredients and simmer 15 minutes over moderate heat. Serve the sauce slightly warm, in little bowls. Dunk the satay in this wonderful tangy sauce.

If this recipe is to be served for dinner, rice and sliced cucumbers are a traditional accompaniment. The recipe will serve 2 for dinner, or 4 if used as an appetizer.

3/4 cup Spanish peanuts

4 T. lemon juice

2 T. molasses or brown sugar

*1 tsp. dried minced chili peppers or
   1 tsp. chili powder*

1 tsp. grated fresh ginger

1/2 cup soy sauce

1 cup water

2 cloves garlic, minced

Pacific Picnic Roast Beef

Pacific Beef is a terrific main dish for a picnic menu. It is both elegant and delicious. You might serve part of the roast hot for dinner and chill the remaining section for the picnic. The beef may also be sliced for lunch sandwiches, and frozen in little packets.

In a bowl that will hold the roast, mix together the soy sauce, garlic, ginger, oil, and sherry. Place the roast in the bowl with the marinade and turn it so all parts are coated. Marinate at least 4 hours or overnight.

Place two inches of water in a shallow roasting pan. Place the roast on a rack in the pan. The liquid should not touch the roast. Bake uncovered at 325° until the meat registers rare to medium rare on a meat thermometer. This

> 1 3 to 4 lb sirloin tip roast
> 1/2 cup soy sauce
> 2 cloves of garlic, minced
> 2 T. fresh ginger, minced
> 2 T. sesame oil
> 1/4 cup sherry
> fresh cilantro for garnish

will take about an hour or an hour and a half. During the roasting, baste with the marinade, letting it drip in the water for flavor fumes. Be sure to maintain the water level, adding more liquid if necessary. It is this combination of marinating and steam roasting that makes the roast so tender and delicious.

For the picnic, chill the beef, slice it thinly, and garnish with fresh cilantro. This will serve 6.

Beef Brisket with Polynesian Flavors

There is a kind of passion in California for flavors reminiscent of the Pacific islands. Restaurants use Polynesian decor and serve tropical drinks with orchids hanging over the edge of the glass. California is, of course, on the edge of the Pacific, and it is only natural that it should be influenced by these exotic flavors. One of the best recipes to come from the island cultures is this one for brisket. Traditionally, it is served hot, but you may also serve it sliced cold for a picnic or for dinner on a hot summer day.

Place the brisket in a bowl or shallow pan. Mix together the remaining ingredients and pour over the brisket. Make sure all parts of the meat are covered. Refrigerate at least 4 hours, or preferably overnight.

Place the brisket in a baking pan with the marinade. Cover tightly with a double layer

1 4–5 lb beef brisket
1 cup soy sauce
1/2 cup dry sherry
1/2 cup brown sugar
1 cup orange, lemon, or pineapple juice
2 cloves of garlic, peeled and minced
salt and pepper to taste
2 T. freshly grated ginger or
    1 T. dried ginger
1 cup fresh or canned pineapple, diced
    for garnish

of foil. Bake at 325° for 3 to 3-1/2 hours, until tender. Check during the baking to make sure there is enough liquid; if not, add extra soy sauce or fruit juice, being sure to replace the foil tightly.

Remove meat from juices. Slice and serve with warmed pan juices and garnished with pineapple. Serve to 4 or 5, with hot steamed rice.

Shepherd's Pie

What is a traditional food from London doing in a California cookbook? I have included it for sentimental reasons.

I had a wonderful home economics teacher, Mrs. Armstrong, who was a favorite at our Audubon Junior High School in Southwest Los Angeles. She was cheery, and if food ingredients were accidentally spilled she stayed calm. It was her philosophy that students needed to know how to use ground beef in many ways. Shepherd's pie was my very favorite. I rushed home and made it for the family dinner. I made it for my friends, and when I got married I made it for my husband, who was at that time a student. It is a good budget dish.

The name of the dish fascinated me, and as I became more interested in food trivia I discovered that the dish really was originally made for shepherds. It could easily be kept warm and waiting, as lambs do go astray and the shepherds might be late coming home. There are variations on shepherd's pie; sometimes lamb or leftover roast beef are

2 T. butter or vegetable oil
1 large onion, chopped
1 clove of garlic, minced
1 medium sized carrot, finely diced
1 lb ground beef
1/2 cup dry white wine
1/2 cup water or broth
salt and pepper to taste
1/2 tsp. dried thyme
1 T. flour
2 cups mashed potatoes
1/2 cup grated cheddar for topping

used. Basically, it is simply a dish of meat with a covering of mashed potatoes. I have found that the addition of a little wine is a tasty touch.

Heat the butter or oil in a skillet. Brown the onion, carrot, and garlic just until limp. Add the ground beef, and cook just until lightly browned. Sprinkle in the flour and stir, adding salt, pepper, and thyme. Now add wine and broth or water. Simmer for 10 minutes.

Lightly grease a 9-inch square or similar size baking pan. Fill with the meat mixture. Spoon mashed potatoes on top. Sprinkle with the cheese, and bake at 350° for 30 minutes. This will serve 4.

Russian River Cabbage Rolls

Russians came to California in pursuit of the sea otter, and were among the first settlers on the Northern California Coast. Their colony was called Rossiya, and is now the Fort Ross State Historical Park. Two-lane roads meander among oak covered hills as the Russian River winds along to the sea and the road to Fort Ross.

Cabbage rolls are among the traditional Russian favorite foods, and have long since become part of the California cuisine.

Heat water in a pot large enough to hold the head of cabbage. When it is boiling, add the cabbage. Cover and simmer for 10 minutes. Drain the cabbage and, when cool enough to handle, remove 12 of the largest leaves. The remainder of the cabbage can be used for soup.

In a frying pan, melt the drippings (or oil). Gently fry the onions and garlic just until limp. Mix the beef in a bowl with the salt,

(continued on next page)

(continued from previous page)

pepper, parsley, lemon juice, egg, cooked onion, and garlic. Blend well. This will be the cabbage rolls' stuffing.

Fill each leaf with a heaping tablespoon of the stuffing. Roll the leaf around the filling, using a toothpick to hold together if necessary.

Melt the butter in a frying pan. Brown the rolls lightly. Carefully place the rolls in a flat baking dish. Blend the flour into the juice remaining in the pan, stirring to make a smooth paste. Add tomatoes, wine, and sour cream. Cook for a minute, to blend. Pour this sauce over the rolls in the baking dish. Cover and bake at 325° for 45 minutes. Hot steamed rice or mashed potatoes will go well with this Russian treat. It will serve 4–5.

1 large head of cabbage
1 lb lean ground beef
1 T. bacon drippings (or vegetable oil)
1 medium onion, chopped
1 clove garlic, minced
2 T. parsley
salt and pepper to taste
juice of 1/2 lemon
1 egg
4 T. butter
1 T. flour
1 cup solid pack tomatoes
1/2 cup dry red wine
1 cup sour cream

Sobon Estate Picnic Roman Meat Cakes

In the gold country of California, there are many ancient, gnarled grapevines more than a century old. Some miners found a life of growing grapes and producing wines more pleasant than the rigors of mining. The Sobon Estate winery, formerly the D'Agostini winery, dates back to 1856. One early spring while visiting Sobon, we sat among the pale green grass and spring flowers and had a delightful picnic nibbling on these Roman meat cakes.

Lightly beat the egg in a medium sized bowl. Stir in the wine. Crumble bread into this mixture and let stand a few minutes to absorb the liquid. Add remaining ingredients to the bowl and blend together.

1 lb lean ground beef
1 egg
1/4 cup red or white wine
1 slice of white bread
2 tsp. minced parsley
salt and pepper to taste
grated rind of 1 medium lemon
1 clove of garlic, minced
olive oil for frying
*lemon wedges and minced parsley
    for garnish*

Form the meat into flat cakes about 1/2″ high and 2-1/2″ in diameter. Heat enough olive oil in a frying pan to permit even frying (a nonstick pan works well). Fry meat patties on each side until golden brown. They may be served hot or cold. Garnish with lemon wedges and parsley. This will make 6 cakes.

Teriyaki Steak

There is a small Japanese restaurant in my neighborhood that has been there for many years. Broiled teriyaki steak with hot steamed rice is one of their most popular offerings. Accompanied by a pot of hot tea, this dinner always makes one feel comfortable and cheerful. It is a flavorful combination that is easy to prepare in your home kitchen.

Cut the steak into four serving pieces and place them in a flat dish. Mix the remaining ingredients together and pour over the meat, stirring around so each piece is coated. Marinate at least 4 hours, or overnight. The meat may also be cut into cubes for cooking on skewers.

2 lb top sirloin steak (boneless fish or poultry may also be used)
1 T. crushed fresh ginger
1 clove of garlic, minced
2 T. brown sugar
2 T. sesame oil

To cook, remove from the sauce, place under a broiler and cook to desired doneness, turning once. This can also be prepared on an outside barbecue—dribble the remaining sauce over the meat before cooking. This makes enough for 4. Serve with hot steamed rice. A few lime slices make an attractive garnish.

Holiday Tamales

Serving hot steaming tamales has become a California tradition for the Christmas holidays. They were brought to California from Mexico centuries ago (the word tamale comes from the Nahuatl word tamalii). Corn is a main ingredient of the Mexican cuisine, and sixteenth-century Spanish chroniclers wrote about the many types of tamales they saw during their conquest of Mexico.

One of the pleasures of making tamales is that you need friends and family to help you assemble them. This is fun. Sometimes we sip a beer or a glass of wine to add to the festivity of the preparation. My neighbor, who taught me all about tamales many years ago, said extra tamales should always be made, as it is the custom to send a bowl of hot tamales to the house of a friend.

You will need a big steamer to prepare these; a tamale pot if you have one, or you can just use a very large kettle with a steamer basket.

Step One—The Filling (for 50–60 tamales)

4–5 lb pork shoulder, beef chuck, chicken, or turkey, cut in large chunks

2 T. vegetable oil or lard

3 cloves garlic, minced

2 onions, sliced

4 T. chili powder

2 28-oz. cans of tomato puree

3–4 cups of water, to cover meat or poultry

salt and pepper to taste

I have found it best to prepare this filling a day or two ahead, to allow the meat or poultry to absorb the flavor of the sauce.

Heat the oil in a large soup or stew pot. Sauté the onion and garlic in the oil just until they become transparent (do not brown). Add meat or poultry. Stir around with onions and garlic, then add remaining ingredients. Cover and cook until the meat is very tender. The time will vary depending upon the meat that is used. If the liquid gets low, add additional water. Cool and refrigerate until needed.

Step Two—The Corn Husks

1-1/2 lb dried corn husks

Several hours before you are ready to assemble the tamales, soak the corn husks in water. I put mine in the kitchen sink (cleaned first, of course) or in a large roasting pan. Hold them down with a weight of some kind. You will need to separate them as they soak. Swish the husks around in the water every now and then. It is important that the water reach all parts of the husks

Step Three—The Masa

5 lb of prepared masa

The easy way to do this is to order it a day ahead from a Mexican grocery store. If you do not have a Mexican grocery store around, you can buy masa harina, made by Quaker

Oats. Prepare it yourself according to the package directions.

Step Four—The Olives

2 cans of black olives (drained weight 6 oz.)

Drain the olives and set them aside.

Step Five—The Assembly, or "Tamalada" ("Tamale Party")

Remove the meat or poultry from the sauce. Shred into little strips, removing any bone pieces. Return to sauce.

Drain the corn husks and spread them out so you can be selective. Tear some of the husks into strips about 1/3 inch wide. Tie two of these strips together, end to end, to make one long strand. These are your "ties" and you will need one for each tamale.

Select a spot where you have some elbow room, such as a table or long drainboard. Set out your corn husks, masa, filling, and olives, all in a row. Take a large corn husk, about 5 inches or wider (if the husk is narrow, use two overlapping husks). Spread the husk with 2 T. of the masa. Place 2 T. of the filling on top of the masa. Top with an olive. Fold one side over and then fold the second side over. Fold each end up so they overlap. It's like wrapping a package. Tie with the corn husk "tie".

Place the tamales in a steamer and steam for one hour. Do not let the water dry up or get too low, as the steam is what is cooking the tamales.

Step Six—The Feast

Remove the tamales, serve, and enjoy. Do not worry if you have a little masa, a few olives, or extra husks left over. Making tamales is not an exact science.

Olvera Street Carnitas with Salsa

Olvera Street is a colorful pedestrian walkway known as "The Birthplace of Los Angeles." It was on this site that the original settlers made their first permanent encampment in Los Angeles, and the street has been preserved as a historic landmark. Lined with shops and restaurants specializing in Mexican gifts and foods, it is a favorite field trip for school children in Los Angeles. My children would always return with sticky jewel-colored suckers or a delicate hand-blown glass animal. Tantalizing scents assail you from all sides, inviting you to dine on Olvera Street and enjoy the traditional foods of early California. I adore carnitas folded into a fresh soft tortilla, and often prepare them at home. Carnitas, in Spanish, simply means "little pieces of meat." Serve them with salsa or guacamole.

(continued on next page)

(continued from previous page)

> *3 lb of pork shoulder or other cut of pork*
> *salt and pepper to taste*
> *2 T. chili powder*
> *1 T. cumin seed or powder*
> *cilantro and lime wedges for garnish*
>   *(optional)*

Cut the pork in 1-1/2″ cubes. Pork for this dish should have a little fat, as this produces the crispy character of the dish. Place the pork cubes on a shallow, lightly greased baking pan, and sprinkle with salt, pepper, chili, and cumin. Bake in a 325° oven for one hour, stirring now and then. Drain and serve on a warmed platter with garnishes and salsa (see next recipe) or guacamole.

Fresh Salsa

There are many salsa recipes (see the "Zestful Accompaniments" chapter for more variations). The following is a simple recipe that merely provides a guide; more or less of any ingredient may be used according to your taste. Remember to use caution when you cook with chiles. Wash your hands after preparing chiles, and NEVER rub your eyes while you are working with chiles.

> *3 medium tomatoes, peeled and chopped*
> *1 onion, peeled and chopped*
> *1 clove of garlic, peeled and chopped*
> *2 tsp. vinegar or lime juice*
> *2 Anaheim chiles, chopped finely*
> *2 T. fresh minced cilantro*

Mix all ingredients together. Let stand for half an hour so flavors can mellow. Jalapeño or serrano chiles may be added for extra hotness.

Beef and Pineapple on a Skewer

Skewer cooking has always been the rage in this multicultural state, from the first Indian inhabitants along the coast who impaled bits of fish over a campfire, to sophisticated city diners who appreciate the wonderful flavor melange that is possible with skewer cooking. Skewer combinations can be complex, but one of the best is this simple blend of juicy pineapple with steak cubes. This recipe may be enlarged for a party and cooked on an outside barbecue.

Cut the beef in bite-sized cubes (about 3/4″ × 3/4″). Mix the remaining ingredients, except pineapple. Marinate the beef overnight, or for at least an hour. Remove from marinade. Reserve marinade.

1 lb top sirloin steak
1/4 cup soy sauce
2 T. brown sugar
1 clove of garlic, finely minced
1 tsp. freshly grated ginger
1 T. sesame or peanut oil
1 cup fresh pineapple, cut in cubes, or one 8-1/4 oz. can, drained

Thread meat on skewers, alternating with pineapple cubes. If you use bamboo skewers, soak them in cold water for at least 20 minutes before using. Broil or barbecue until meat is cooked to desired doneness. Baste with reserved marinade while cooking. These are delicious on a bed of hot rice, and this recipe will serve 2.

Chinese Barbecued Pork (Char Siu)

My father had a passion for Chinese restaurants. It was like a game for him to see how many people he could gather for a Los Angeles Chinatown dinner. It is a practice in Chinese restaurants that an additional dish is provided free for every four persons in the group. With four, you may get free eggs foo yung, and with eight people you may get not only eggs foo yung, but perhaps a platter of this marvelous Chinese barbecued pork, Char Siu.

The table would be jammed with delectable varieties of Chinese food on plates with pretty oriental designs. We would all drink perfumed tea and finish with crunchy fortune cookies that contained curious cautions about our futures.

Char Siu can be made at home and may be served cold for picnics, hot with cilantro sprigs, or as an addition to stir-fry dishes. It may be frozen in batches for convenience.

3–4 lb pork, tenderloin or butt section
3 T. soy sauce
6 T. ketchup
2 T. honey
2 garlic cloves, finely chopped
1 T. fresh ginger, finely minced
1 T. sherry or white wine
1 T. peanut oil or other oil
cilantro for garnish

Mix all the ingredients, except the pork and cilantro, together in a bowl. Cut the pork into strips approximately 4″ × 2″ × 1″. Place in the bowl with the marinade and refrigerate overnight, or at least four hours.

Line a large roasting pan with foil. Pour one cup of water into the pan. Drain the pork, reserving the marinade. Lay the pork strips on a baking rack and place in the pan. Bake at 375° for 40 minutes, basting several times with reserved marinade. Turn oven to 450° and cook an additional 10 minutes. Serve hot from the oven garnished with cilantro. This will serve 6.

Butterflied Lamb Barbecue

Unlike other states, California has no particular barbecue season. Year-round, it is one of the most popular ways of cooking in this state. Charcoal and the latest in barbecue equipment are always on sale, with the markets offering free recipes for the latest trends in over-the-coals cooking.

One of the finest and most delicious meats to barbecue is a boned leg of lamb. It is called butterflied lamb because after the meat is boned and spread out it looks (with imagination) rather like a large butterfly.

Ask your butcher to bone the leg of lamb for you. It should be left in one piece. Place the lamb in a large, shallow, stainless steel container. Blend remaining ingredients and pour over the lamb, stirring around so all parts of the meat are covered. Marinate overnight or at least 4 hours. Turn the meat once or twice for better absorption of the marinade.

1 5–7 lb leg of lamb, boned and "butterflied"

2 cloves of garlic, peeled and minced

3/4 cup olive oil

1/4 cup red wine vinegar

1 medium onion, chopped

2 tsp. Dijon-style mustard

salt and pepper to taste

fresh herbs of your choice, rosemary or basil (about 1/2 cup)

When ready to barbecue, remove the meat from the marinade, and dry it with paper towels. Reserve the marinade. Place lamb on the barbecue rack, fat skin side up. Baste with marinade. Turn once while grilling. The cooking time will be about 10–15 minutes per pound. Lamb should be served slightly pink inside. This will serve 6. Serve with hot steamed rice and your favorite mixed green salad. Red wine (or rosé) is a preferred accompaniment.

Braised Veal Shanks

One might say that a "bone craze" is spreading across California. It is simply a return to the basic enjoyment of picking up a bone and gnawing on it. For some years this pleasure was put aside in favor of a dainty nouvelle trend, but fortunately, Californians are rediscovering foods that are fun. This dish of Italian origin is called osso bucco, which means hollow bones. The hollow contains marrow, which, in Italy, is considered a delicacy and eaten with a special fork designed to reach down into the interior of the bone. The shanks are traditionally garnished with a lemon, parsley, and garlic combination called gremolada. I have served this at fall and winter dinners, with rice and lots of bread to dip in the flavorful juices. If you can, make this a day ahead for the flavors to mellow.

Dust the shanks with flour. Heat the oil and butter in a large stew pot. Brown the shanks on all sides, being careful not to break the marrow. Usually it is best to do this browning in batches and not all at once. The

4 veal shanks, about 4–5 lb, cut in 2-1/2 inch lengths

1/3 cup flour

2 T. butter

2 T. olive oil

1 medium onion, chopped

2 carrots, chopped

2 stalks of celery, diced

2 garlic cloves, peeled and minced

salt and pepper to taste

1/2 tsp. thyme

1 bay leaf

1 28-oz. can of tomato puree or whole tomatoes

3/4 cup white wine

shanks should be dark and crusty looking when you finish.

Remove the shanks, and add the vegetables to the pan. Add a little more olive oil if needed. Fry just until limp. Add tomatoes, seasonings, and white wine.

Return the shanks to the pot, placing them upright to keep the marrow intact. Cook over a low flame or in a 325° oven until the veal is tender. This will take 1-1/2 to 2 hours.

The finishing touch to osso bucco is the gremolada. Combine the grated rind of 1 lemon, 2 T. finely chopped parsley, and 1 clove of minced garlic. Stir into the sauce and cook another few minutes. Serve to 4, with the shanks upright and sauce dribbled over the tops.

Pasta and Rice

Main Dishes or Meal Accompaniments

Where would California cuisine be without pasta and rice? These staples fill many dining needs and tastes. Our ethnically diverse population prepares these two favorite foods in a variety of exciting ways. Rice might be combined with green chiles, sour cream, and cheese, and baked for a winning dish. Pasta is popular with everyone and has its place in the state's history. Macaroni and cheese filled many an early California pioneer's stomach.

Rice is a leading California crop, and many varieties of pasta fill the supermarket shelves. Many California cooks have pasta machines and enjoy making pasta at home. Pasta and rice have many health benefits and remain very popular foods.

Santa Barbara Mission Chili Rice

Green chiles and rice are a favorite combination dating back to the California mission days. Chiles grow very well in this warm dry climate, and when the Santa Barbara Mission was completed in 1786 it had a bounteous fruit and vegetable garden to feed the neophytes and mission staff. Even today, when you visit this "Queen of the Missions" you can see the remains of the garden.

This modern version of the classic dish always wins raves in my cooking classes. It is terrific for barbecue dinners or potlucks. If you tuck a few bay shrimp, chicken pieces, or shredded pork into the casserole, it can be a main dish.

3 cups cooked rice (1 cup uncooked)
1 tsp. chili powder
1 tsp. cumin seed or cumin powder (optional)
1 tsp. salt
1 6-oz. can diced green chiles (or 4 fresh peeled chiles), minced
2 cups sour cream
2 cups grated Jack or cheddar cheese
1 tsp. oil

Cook the rice by your favorite method. Cool slightly and add the chili, cumin, and salt. Mix in the sour cream and stir well. Lightly grease a 1-1/2 quart baking dish with the oil. Place half the rice, half the green chiles and half the cheese in layers. Repeat, ending with the cheese. Bake in a 350° oven for 25 minutes, uncovered. Garnish, if desired, with fresh cilantro, sliced tomatoes, or a few sliced olives. This will serve 6.

Spanish Rice

The "Spanish rice" recipes that have been used by generations of Californians are not really from Spain. Spanish rice is a unique California mixture, a little bit of Spain and Mexico and the Golden State all mixed together. It is one of those comfy homey things your mother used to make for a supper main dish. Perhaps it is not as popular now as in former times, and can use a revival.

Place the bacon and olive oil in a 2-quart oven proof casserole or saucepan over a medium flame. As soon as the bacon begins to sizzle, add the onion, pepper or chili, and rice. Stir-fry until rice is glossy. Add the tomatoes, salt and pepper, and water. Break up any large pieces of tomato. I use a pair of scissors and sort of snip them. Add oregano,

1–2 slices of raw bacon, cut in 1/2″ pieces

1 T. olive oil

1 medium onion, chopped

1/2 green bell pepper, chopped, or 2 T. diced green chiles

1 16-oz. can whole peeled tomatoes

salt and pepper to taste

1 cup water

1/2 tsp. dried oregano (optional)

1/2 cup grated cheddar cheese

if used. Give a stir to blend the ingredients, cover, and place in a 350° oven for 40 minutes. Remove cover, sprinkle on cheese, and bake for an additional 10 minutes. This will serve 4 generously.

Indonesian Fried Rice

I first tasted this delicious rice combination on a Dutch ship. My husband and I were on our way to school in France in our early married days. As our funds were very limited, we needed to travel as inexpensively as possible. The cheapest transportation we could find was a troopship from World War II that had been converted to a dormitory passenger ship. Men slept in one part and the ladies in another section. There were hammock-like bunks and strange community showers. It was far from luxurious, but the food was quite interesting. Some of the crew were Indonesian and they liked to serve Nasi Goreng. I was quite taken with all the flavors and was able to get the recipe from one of the cooks. When we returned to California this dish became one of my favorites for dinner party menus.

Lightly brown the onion and garlic in the peanut oil just until limp. Add the rice and

1/3 cup oil (peanut or vegetable) for frying
2 chopped onions
1 clove garlic, minced
4 cups cooked rice, cooled
1 tsp. cumin, whole or ground
1/2 tsp. dried red pepper flakes
2 cups cooked chicken, cubed
1 cup cooked bay shrimp
1 cup crab meat (optional)
1/2 cup cubed ham

remaining ingredients. It is important that the rice be cold before frying, so it is best to make the rice ahead and refrigerate over night. Stir fry until blended and hot. This will take about 10 minutes. Be sure not to overcook. Serve at once. This will serve 6 generously. Beer is the preferred accompanying beverage.

114

Rice Pilaf

Rice pilaf is the parent of the famed San Francisco Rice-a-Roni™. This dish originated in the Middle East, where rice combined with thin noodles is a mainstay of the cuisine.

You can buy the cute box with the cable car on it, suggesting the culinary reputation of San Francisco, but if you have a little time, try this traditional pilaf.

> 4 T. butter
>
> 1/2 cup vermicelli or other fine noodles
>
> 1 cup long grain rice
>
> salt and pepper to taste
>
> 2 cups chicken broth (1/4 cup may be white wine)

Melt the butter in a saucepan. Break the noodles in 1/2- to 1/4-inch pieces. Add the noodles and rice to the pan. Stir around in the butter until glazed and very lightly browned. Add liquid, salt, and pepper to blend. Cover and cook over a low flame for 25 minutes, or bake in a 350° oven for 30 minutes (I prefer the oven method). Fluff rice with a fork before serving. This will make 4 servings.

Mushroom Lasagna

Lasagna is a popular dish, and a favorite for dinner parties. My friends Becky and Eddie celebrated their 25th wedding anniversary by inviting about 45 friends for a dinner. They made trays and trays of lasagna ahead of time, and froze them. The day of the party they baked the lasagna in their own and neighbors' ovens. All the preparation had been done ahead, so the host and hostess were able to visit with their friends.

The word lasagna comes from the Latin word lasanum, meaning "pot," which makes sense because lasagna is baked in a sort of pot. This lasagna version is meatless. Its flavor comes from fresh mushrooms.

Heat the olive oil in a large saucepan. Add onion, garlic and mushrooms. Fry just until the vegetables are slightly limp. Do not brown. Add the tomato sauce and canned tomatoes (breaking up any large pieces), wine, salt, and pepper. Simmer uncovered, stirring now and then, for 30 minutes. Cool and refrigerate. This may be done a day or

(continued from previous page)

two ahead. This is a good basic sauce and can be used as a topping for any pasta.

To prepare lasagna, beat the eggs lightly and mix with the ricotta cheese. Blend in parsley. Cook the noodles as per package directions. Lightly oil a 3 to 3-1/2 qt. baking pan with a little olive oil. Place 3 T. of the sauce in the bottom of the pan. Place a layer of noodles followed by a layer of the sauce. Plop little dabs of the ricotta mixture next, then sprinkle with parmesan followed by slices of mozzarella. Repeat the procedure until all ingredients are used. Bake uncovered in a 350° oven for 30–40 minutes, until hot and bubbling. Let stand a few minutes before cutting into squares. This will make six generous servings. Remember to add an extra 15 minutes or so to the baking time, if the dish has been made ahead and refrigerated.

2 T. olive oil

1 peeled onion, minced

1 clove garlic, minced

2 cups fresh mushrooms, coarsely chopped

1 8-oz. can tomato sauce

1 28-oz. can of tomatoes (solid pack or diced)

1/4 cup red or white wine

salt and pepper to taste

2 eggs

2 cups ricotta cheese (or small curd cottage cheese)

2 T. fresh minced parsley

1/2 lb lasagna noodles (green or white)

1-1/2 cups grated Parmesan cheese

2 cups sliced Mozzarella cheese

Luisa Tetrazzini's Chicken and Pasta Casserole

The famous opera singer Luisa Tetrazzini made her debut in San Francisco. She loved the city and the city loved her, and she returned for every opera season.

Luisa was known not only for her beautiful coloratura voice, but also for her passion for feasting. Her after-the-opera parties were unrivaled. This recipe combining chicken and pasta is one of her creations. It can be made ahead and popped in the oven while guests enjoy conversation, antipasto, and wine.

Cook the spaghettini as per package directions to "al dente." Do not let it become mushy. Drain and set aside.

Melt the butter in a saucepan. Blend in the flour and cook together a minute. Slowly add the half-and-half, stirring until the mixture is slightly thickened (this is a thin sauce). Add the salt, pepper, and cayenne.

1/2 lb (8 oz.) spaghettini
1/3 cup butter
3 T. flour
2 cups half-and-half
salt and pepper to taste
1/4 tsp. cayenne pepper (optional)
1 medium green bell pepper, chopped
3/4 lb mushrooms, thinly sliced
3 cups diced and cooked boneless chicken breast or other parts
3 T. sherry
1 cup grated Parmesan cheese
minced parsley for garnish

Stir in the green pepper, mushrooms, chicken, and sherry. Blend well and set aside.

Lightly butter a 3-quart baking dish. Place the pasta on the bottom, and pour the chicken sauce on top. Sprinkle with the Parmesan. Cook uncovered in a 350° oven for 45 minutes. If you make Luisa's casserole ahead of time and refrigerate it, allow 15–20 minutes extra for baking. Garnish with minced parsley. This will serve 6 generously.

Zesty Eggplant Sauce for Pasta

Eggplant is one of California's most popular vegetables. In the summer, outdoor farmers' markets are filled with piles of these beautiful glossy vegetables. Eggplant has many delicious uses, and this Sicilian-inspired pasta sauce is one of the best.

Peel the eggplant and cut it into 3/4″ cubes. Of course, the cubes will not come out perfectly, but do the best you can. Place the cubes in a colander. With your hands, rub 1 tsp. salt into the cubes. Let the eggplant drain in the colander for 30 minutes, then take some paper towels and blot it dry. This procedure removes the bitter juices from the eggplant.

Heat the oil in a large skillet. Stir-fry the eggplant and garlic until the eggplant is light brown and limp. Add tomato sauce, red wine, salt and pepper to taste, and red pepper. Simmer over a low flame for another 15 minutes, stirring now and then. Add capers

1 whole eggplant, about 1-1/2 lb
5 T. olive oil
2 garlic cloves, minced
1 15-oz. can of tomato sauce
1 cup dry red wine
salt and pepper to taste
1 tsp. dried red pepper, crushed
1 T. capers
1/4 cup lightly toasted pine nuts (optional)
1 lb spaghetti or other pasta of your choice, cooked according to package directions
freshly grated Parmesan cheese
minced parsley for garnish

and pine nuts (if used). Stir for a minute until blended.

To serve, place some sauce on each portion of cooked pasta, and top with Parmesan and a little minced parsley. This will serve 4–5. The sauce may be made ahead and refrigerated.

Sylvia Sebastiani's Spaghetti Sauce

Over the years, I have tried many spaghetti sauces. This classic recipe, from a California wine country lady, is one of my all-time favorites. It has all the flavor and character you might expect from a true California-Italian kitchen. This versatile sauce can be used with any style of pasta. It is very tasty with penne, but is at its very best with spaghetti.

If using meat, brown it in the olive oil and butter. Add the celery and onions, sauté until brown, then add garlic. Salt and pepper to taste, then add spices, mushrooms with their liquid, tomatoes, and tomato sauce. Rinse the tomato sauce cans with 1-1/2 cups of water, and add to the sauce along with the wine and sugar. Cook for 3 hours over low heat, stirring occasionally. If not using meat, start by browning the onions and celery, and proceed as above.

Instead of ground beef, a piece of pot roast can be used. Brown on all sides and pro-

1 lb ground beef (optional)

4 T. olive oil

4 T. butter

4 stalks celery, chopped

4 onions, chopped

4 cloves garlic, chopped fine

salt and pepper to taste

1/4 tsp. thyme

1/4 tsp. rosemary

1/2 cup finely chopped parsley

1-1/2 cups dried Italian mushrooms (soaked in 1 cup hot water and then chopped)

1 28-oz. can solid pack tomatoes, mashed with liquid

6 8-oz. cans tomato sauce

1-1/2 cups water

1 cup red or white wine (Sebastiani, of course!)

1 tsp. sugar

ceed as above, letting meat simmer in sauce. After two hours, remove from the sauce and keep warm. Slice and serve as a meat course for your dinner. If your family likes their sauce hot, add a small chili pepper, chopped very fine, while the sauce is simmering. These peppers are hot and go a long way, so use them with caution. This recipe yields a quantity of sauce greater than you would normally use at one time, so freeze the remainder in pint jars, filling 3/4 full. I always keep a supply of frozen sauce on hand—it helps put together numerous meals in a short time.

Spaghetti Alla Carbonara

I have been giving cooking classes at the South Bay Adult School for many years. The class cooks a complete dinner, and when it is finished we all sit down and enjoy the food. The students vary in age from early twenties to over 65. Everyone becomes friends while cooking together. There have even been some romances, one that ended in a wedding.

Spaghetti alla carbonara has been one of my most popular recipes. I first tasted it in the Trastevere section of Rome, where the families can trace their roots back for over two thousand years. They call themselves the "True Romans." The need to stretch the food dollar, or in this case, the food lire, has always been there. Trastevere families are hardworking and most have many children to feed.

The beauty of carbonara is that it can easily be made in a few minutes from ingredients (bacon and eggs) that most of us always have

1 lb spaghetti or spaghettini, cooked as per package directions

4 raw eggs, lightly mixed in a bowl

1/2 lb diced cooked bacon, drained

1/4 cup of butter (room temperature)

3 tsp. freshly grated Parmesan or Romano cheese

2 tsp. freshly ground black pepper

in our refrigerators. The name carbonara means "coal." The ground black pepper sprinkled on top, with a little imagination, resembles coal.

Drain the cooked spaghetti. Place in a warmed bowl. Quickly mix in the eggs, bacon, butter, and lastly, the cheese. Divide into four or five portions on warmed plates. Sprinkle with the pepper.

Don't worry, the hot pasta cooks the eggs. Be sure to mix the eggs in a speedy swirling motion so the eggs and bacon cling nicely to the spaghetti. Chilled white wine will add to the Trastevere mood.

California Macaroni and Cheese

In the early days of San Francisco, most of the people in the city were men who needed warm meals and a place to sleep. The many lodging houses competed fiercely for patrons. San Francisco newspapers carried their advertisements on the front pages, with weekly rates and a list of foods served for dinner. Macaroni and cheese, as comforting and pleasantly filling then as now, was always included.

In this version, a little wine is added to give a zippy flavor, as are some optional chopped green chiles. If you wish to make the dish heartier, a cup of diced chicken, ham, or bay shrimp can be mixed into the macaroni before baking.

Cook the pasta as per package directions and drain. Do not overcook.

Melt the butter in a saucepan, add the onion, and cook until just limp. Add the flour and stir until well blended. Slowly add the milk

2 cups elbow macaroni, small mostaccioli, or other small pasta
3 T. butter
1/2 medium onion, chopped (1/4 cup)
3 T. flour
1 cup milk or half-and-half
1/2 cup dry white wine
2 cups grated sharp cheddar cheese
2 T. freshly chopped Anaheim chiles or canned green chiles (optional)
salt and pepper to taste
1/4 tsp. cayenne pepper (optional)

and stir until the sauce is slightly thick. Add the wine (don't worry if the mixture looks a little curdly) and then the cheese, and the chiles, if used. Add the seasonings and stir until the cheese is melted.

Butter a 1-1/2 to 2-quart casserole. Add the drained pasta. Pour the sauce over it and mix with the pasta. Bake at 350° for 25 minutes. A sprinkle of paprika may be added to the top for extra color. This will serve 4.

Penne Pasta in a Hot Pepper Sauce

Pasta is always on California restaurant menus and in our kitchens. In the last few years, penne has become a favorite. The shape is sort of like a stretched-out macaroni, or you might think of it as a part of a quill pen (that is the origin of the Italian word). It is a wonderful shape to look at and to eat. Penne is very attractive on a plate, served either as a main dish or as an accompaniment to one. This version, with a tangy hot sauce, is a winner.

Heat the oil in a large frying pan. Add the salt pork or bacon, garlic and onion, and stir over medium flame until lightly browned. Add the tomatoes, wine, salt, pepper, and red

2 T. olive oil

1/4 lb salt pork or bacon, diced in small pieces

1 clove of garlic, minced

1 onion, chopped

1 16-oz. can solid pack tomatoes, or 2 cups fresh tomatoes, peeled

1/4 cup dry red wine

salt and pepper to taste

1 T. dry red pepper flakes

1/2 lb penne pasta

Parmesan cheese for topping

pepper. Cook, stirring now and then, for 20 minutes. This may be done ahead.

Cook the penne following the package directions. Drain and serve with sauce and cheese on top. This will serve 3.

123

Vegetables

From the State's Bountiful, Fertile Valleys

California leads the nation in vegetable production. Every kind of vegetable can be grown here. Our inland valleys are filled with beautiful, abundant crops.

I always had celery and other vegetable sticks tucked in my school lunches. When my family had company for dinner, my mother always served little chilled bowls of these crunchy vegetables. I was not alone in my celery and carrot crunching, all my friends nibbled on them too. When one neighbor added raw zucchini spears, we thought that was pretty "way out."

My mother liked to have my sister and me help shell peas and lima beans. It was a pleasurable duty to handle those pretty green pods and sniff that honest pleasant vegetable scent. To prepare string beans in our kitchen, we carefully removed the strings and cut the beans in long slivers. My mother said it was French style and we felt very continental eating them. Thanksgiving brought a special peeling of little boiling onions. This was a bit tedious and my eyes watered, but when we sat down to dinner I knew it was worthwhile. A beautiful bowl was filled with creamed onions that looked like large pearls floating in a white sea.

When I was pregnant with my daughter Suzanne, I had an unquenchable desire for artichokes. Some days I would devour four of them. This did not burn out my artichoke passion, for today they remain one of my very favorite things to eat.

.California is the vegetable basket of our country, and this chapter offers some of the ways we use this abundance.

California Carrot Casserole

Carrots are everywhere in California food. A few lightly cooked strips may garnish a dinner plate, or crispy carrot pieces are served as appetizers. In this recipe, the carrots are cooked and combined with flavorful ingredients to make a delicious casserole. This colorfully festive dish adds a bright taste to a holiday table.

Cut the carrots in small pieces. Cover with lightly salted water and cook, covered, until tender, about 10 minutes. Drain and mash coarsely. Place the carrots in a bowl. Add the

3–4 carrots
4 whole green onions, minced
1 cup cheddar cheese, grated
salt and pepper to taste
2 eggs, beaten
butter
paprika and minced parsley for garnish

remaining ingredients and blend. Place the mixture in a lightly buttered casserole. Dot with butter.

Bake at 350° for 20 minutes. Garnish with paprika and minced parsley. This will serve four.

Crispy Garlic String Beans

1 lb fresh green string beans
2 T. butter
1 clove garlic, finely minced
salt and pepper to taste
1 tsp. fresh lemon juice

In California, we do not like overcooked vegetables, especially string beans. This was not always true—canned string beans used to be popular before World War II. Canned vegetables were sort of a novelty, but once fresh string beans began to appear in markets all over the state, who could really want a canned product? This style of preparing them makes them a real treat. Crisp green, with garlic and butter, they are a joy anytime.

Wash the beans and cut in several slices lengthwise, discarding stem tip. Plunge the beans in a quart (yes, a quart) of boiling salted water. Cook for 8 minutes, or just until barely tender. Remove from water, drain, and rinse with cold water immediately. This will preserve the color and stop the cooking process. This step may be done ahead.

Melt the butter in a frying pan. Stir in the garlic and lemon juice. Toss in the green beans and stir just long enough to coat and heat. Serve immediately! This green delight will serve 4.

Delicato Marinated Onions

Delicato's marinated onions make a wonderful relish to serve with ham, and are terrific on a ham on rye sandwich. This recipe, from Delicato cookbook author Arlene Mueller, will add a special touch to any party table.

Place onions, salt, and pepper in wine. Chill for several hours or overnight. Garnish with parsley sprigs. This will make 4 cups.

4 cups very thinly sliced Bermuda onions
1 tsp. salt
1/8 tsp. white pepper
2 cups dry white wine
Parsley sprigs for garnish

For a brighter, rosier look, substitute red onions and Rosé or Cabernet wine, and use plenty of grated black pepper.

Uncomplicated Creamed Spinach

Creamed spinach has a pretty green-flecked look, tastes wonderful, and adds class to any dinner. Unfortunately, most recipes for creamed spinach are complicated, involving sauces with many ingredients, made in separate pans and requiring careful stirring and timing. A friend served this with a salmon dinner, and when everyone complimented her on the creamed spinach she shared her quick and easy recipe.

If the spinach is fresh, remove stems, wash well, and cook covered in a saucepan with about 1/8 cup of salted water for 6 minutes. If frozen, cook as per package directions.

1 bunch of fresh spinach (or 1 10-oz. pkg. frozen chopped spinach)

1 4-oz. pkg. cream cheese, at room temperature

salt and pepper to taste

pinch of nutmeg or 1 tsp. minced onion (optional)

Drain spinach well, squeezing to remove excess liquid. Lightly butter an oven casserole. Mix the cream cheese, salt, and pepper with the spinach. Combine well to make a smooth mixture. Some cooks like to add a dash of nutmeg or a teaspoon of minced onion. Bake at 350° for 10–12 minutes, uncovered. This will make 4 medium portions.

Roman-style Eggplant Parmesan

In summer, the street markets of Rome are filled with shiny, glossy purple eggplants. When I lived there, a neighbor taught me how to prepare this classic summer dish. It became a favorite of our family.

In California, summertime also brings beautiful ripe eggplants, grown in the hot California valleys. Eggplant Parmesan, served warm for best flavor, is most satisfying for a light summer dinner. Cooled, it can also be a delightful picnic dish.

Slice the eggplant crosswise in thin slices. Do not peel. Dip each slice in the beaten egg, and then in the crumbs or meal. Heat the olive oil in a frying pan, about 1/4 cup to begin with. Fry the eggplant slices until light brown on both sides. A nonstick pan will work well for this procedure. Add more oil as needed. Do not crowd the slices as you fry them. This will take a little time, but unless each slice is nicely fried your dish will not look or taste right. Salt and pepper the slices as you fry them. As each batch is done, remove and drain on paper towels.

2 eggplants, medium size
3 eggs, slightly beaten
cracker meal or fine bread crumbs
olive oil for frying
salt and pepper to taste
4 cups tomato sauce
1/4 cup Mozzarella cheese, sliced thin
1 cup grated Parmesan cheese

You may use a ready-made tomato sauce, or make your own as follows: In 2 T. olive oil, lightly fry 1 chopped onion and 1 minced clove of garlic, just until limp. Add 1 28-oz. can of tomato puree, salt and pepper to taste, and 1 tsp dried or fresh rosemary or basil. Simmer, uncovered, about 1 hour.

Rub a 3-quart (or close) flat baking dish with olive oil. First, make a thin layer of the tomato sauce, then eggplant, followed by the Mozzarella and Parmesan. Repeat the layers until everything is used up. The dish may be refrigerated at this point, if desired.

Bake at 350° for 30 minutes, adding 10 minutes if the dish is cold. This will serve 6 generously.

Mushrooms with Garlic

Mushrooms seem to continue to gain popularity, and California markets are full of them. When you buy fresh mushrooms, select those that have a cap that is tight to the stem. As a mushroom ages, the cap opens and spreads away from the stem.

This is an easy way to prepare delicious mushrooms. They may be served hot from the pan, or at room temperature. Any extra mushrooms may be served in a salad, sandwich, or pizza.

1 lb medium sized mushrooms, sliced
2 cloves of garlic, peeled and minced
2 T. olive oil
salt and pepper to taste
1/2 tsp. dried red pepper (optional)
1/4 cup white wine

In a frying pan (nonstick may be used), warm the olive oil. Add the mushrooms to the pan along with the garlic. Season with salt, pepper, and the red pepper, if used. Stir-fry for just a few minutes, until the mushrooms are cooked, but not overdone. Add the white wine to the pan and give another stir around to blend flavors. Serve as desired.

Grandpa's Mashed Potatoes

6 medium sized russet potatoes
1/2 to 1 cup warmed half-and-half
  or milk
salt and pepper to taste
4–6 T. butter

Mashed potatoes always bring me sentimental memories of early childhood. My grandpa made them a lot, and so did my mother. In my grandparents' Hermosa Beach kitchen, they had one of those old black stoves with a high back and a shelf on the top for storing salt, pepper, and matches. The gas burners had to be lit with a match. Grandpa would cook the potatoes in a big soup pot. When they were almost done, he would heat some milk or cream in a saucepan. The potatoes were drained, leaving a little dab of hot potato water. Next Grandpa would mix the potatoes vigorously with a wooden spoon, adding the hot milk, seasonings, and quite a bit of butter. He always served them to me with an extra dollop of golden butter nestled on the top. They were the best thing in the world.

Mashed potatoes have recently had a new wave of popularity in California restaurants. Trendy spots are adding curious ingredients and presenting them in glorious swirls and shapes. They are interesting and they are fun, but none taste as good as Grandpa's.

Peel the potatoes, cover with lightly salted water, and cook, uncovered, over medium heat until tender. Heat the milk or half-and-half to just hot. Do not boil.

When the potatoes are tender, drain, leaving a dab of potato water. With a wooden spoon or electric mixer, mash the potatoes, adding liquid until desired consistency is reached. Add salt and pepper to taste. Sometimes a dash of nutmeg is added. Dot with butter and serve at once to 6.

Additional ingredients such as mashed garlic, drained chopped spinach, cream cheese, sour cream, olive oil, chopped olives, or diced chiles are often added by creative chefs.

Honeymoon Harvard Beets

One foggy June morning I drove up the California coast with my husband. We had been married just the day before, and we were off to Carmel-by-the-Sea for our honeymoon. It was the first time we had been totally alone in a situation where we did not have to return to our parents' homes to sleep. We were on our own and it was quite exciting. When you leave San Simeon on Highway One, the road winds and climbs along the coast. The ocean views are dramatic and spectacular. We would park at viewing turnouts to hold hands and look at the sea below. It was the first time either of us had seen this part of the California coast.

When we arrived at the Lobos Lodge cottages, we were hungry after the long drive. Across the street, the Pine Cone Inn beckoned to evening diners. We could see candles on the tables and pine branches hung low across the windows. It was our first married dinner and on the menu were Harvard beets. I had never tasted them before. They seemed

3 cups cooked and peeled sliced beets
1/2 cup sugar
1-1/2 tsp. cornstarch
1/4 cup water
1/4 cup white cider vinegar
2 T. butter
2 T. orange marmalade (optional)

to me perfectly marvelous and have been part of my vegetable recipe file ever since.

Combine sugar, cornstarch, water, and vinegar in a saucepan, and cook until slightly thick, stirring to make a smooth mixture. Add butter and blend in. Add beets and heat to serving temperature. Stir in the marmalade. This is a California addition that gives a nice touch. This recipe will serve 6.

Baking beets has also become popular in California. Simply wash and trim the unpeeled beets, leaving one inch of the stem. Wrap with double foil, drizzle a little olive oil in the packet, and bake at 350° for one hour. Let cool in foil. Peel, slice, and serve as desired.

Luther Burbank Scalloped Potatoes

E very California schoolchild learns about Luther Burbank on Arbor day. Schools plant trees, and students give speeches about this plant wizard.

Luther Burbank came to Santa Rosa in 1873 to continue his horticultural career, financing the trip by selling the rights to his "Burbank potato." This energetic man sometimes had 3000 plant experiments going at once. His home in Santa Rosa has been preserved and is open for visitors.

Potatoes are enhanced by white wine in this tasty version of scalloped potatoes. If there are leftovers, they are delicious served cold as a little salad.

Peel the potatoes and cut crossways into slices about 1/3" thick. Divide in thirds.

3–4 medium potatoes, any variety
1/2 lb thinly sliced Swiss cheese
2 medium onions, peeled and sliced
2 T. Dijon-style mustard
salt and pepper to taste
1 cup dry white wine
1/4 cup Parmesan cheese
butter for dish and topping, about 1 T.

Butter a large pie pan (9-1/2" diameter, or 8 × 8" square pan). Lay one third of the potatoes in the dish. Sprinkle with salt and pepper. Spread lightly with half the mustard. Add half the cheese slices, followed by half the onion slices. Repeat another layer of each ingredient, topping with remaining potato slices. Pour wine over dish. Top with Parmesan cheese, dot with butter, cover with foil and bake at 350° for 30 minutes. Remove the foil and bake an additional 20 minutes. This will serve 4 generously.

Rhineland Red Cabbage

One of the sights of Napa Valley is the famous Rhineland House at the Beringer Winery. A replica of a Rhenish family castle, today it serves as a hospitality center for visitors. The winery, founded in 1876, is the oldest in the valley.

This succulent red cabbage, flavored with red wine, is one of the many popular recipes from Germany that have found their way into California cuisine.

Melt the butter or drippings in a heavy saucepan. Add the apple, onion, and sugar. Fry just until limp, about 5 minutes. Add the cabbage, red wine, liquid, and seasonings. Stir together to blend ingredients.

2 T. butter or bacon drippings
1 apple, peeled and sliced
1 onion, sliced
1 T. sugar
1 medium head of red cabbage, sliced thin
1 cup of red wine
1 cup liquid (water or broth)
salt and pepper to taste

Cover and bake in a 325° oven for one hour, or simmer over a low flame on top of the stove. Check the liquid now and then, adding more wine if necessary. This will serve 4–5.

Delicato Broccoli in White Wine

There are vineyards all up and down the state of California. Each one has a character of its own, and climatic variations bring unique flavors to every vineyard. The Delicato Winery is located in Manteca and is over half a century old. This recipe is from Arlene Mueller, co-author of the Delicato cookbook, *Wine, Food and the Good Life.* This is an especially delicious way of preparing broccoli.

Wash broccoli, removing leaves, trimming flowerets, and cutting stems into 1/2-inch pieces. Steam the stem pieces until almost tender (about 15 minutes), then add flowerets and steam until all are tender but not mushy (about 5 minutes).

1 large bunch broccoli
1/2 cup dry white wine
3 T. olive oil
2 garlic cloves, slivered
2 T. lemon juice
2 T. minced parsley

In a separate saucepan, simmer the wine, oil, garlic, lemon juice, and parsley for 10 minutes. Place the broccoli in a heated salad bowl, pour the hot sauce over it, and toss lightly. This will make 4 to 6 portions.

The garlic may be increased in this recipe, if you like. The sauce is also excellent with other vegetables, including boiled potatoes.

Chinatown Stir-Fried Asparagus

1 lb asparagus, washed
2 T. peanut oil (or other cooking oil)
salt and pepper to taste
2 T. soy sauce

Walking is the best way to visit San Francisco's Chinatown. It is an exciting adventure to peek in tiny restaurants, where you will see Chinese chefs stirring food in large woks. This efficient cooking pot was developed in China to quickly cook marvelous combinations of food. This method works wonderfully for fresh asparagus. If you don't own a wok, a frying pan will also work well.

Take each asparagus stalk in your hand and bend it. It will snap off naturally between the tender upper half and woody bottom stem (the bottom stem may be used for soup). Lay the upper stems on a cutting board, and cut them in 1″ pieces on a diagonal.

Heat the oil in a frying pan or wok. Add the asparagus pieces, sprinkle with salt and pepper, give a stir, and cover. Shake the pan a few times as the asparagus is cooking.

After 2 minutes, lift the lid and stir the stems around. Cover and cook for another 3 minutes, shaking the pan from time to time. Uncover, add the soy sauce, and give a final stir. Of course, this may be cooked uncovered, but using a lid creates a little steam which makes the asparagus tender inside and crunchy outside. This will serve 3.

Cooked Cucumbers with Parsley

No California dinner plate is complete without vegetables. Some vegetables are seasonal, and sometimes a sort of new discovery of some overlooked vegetable takes place. In Europe, cucumbers are often cooked and served with a main dish. They are light, with a lovely pale green color. You will be surprised at how tasty and interesting cooked cucumbers are.

Peel the cucumbers. Cut them in half lengthwise, scoop out the seeds with a teaspoon, and cut crosswise into little half-

3 medium cucumbers
salted water
salt and pepper to taste
3 T. butter
1 T. chopped parsley (or mint, if you prefer)

moons about 3/4 of an inch wide. Cook the "moons" in salted water to cover for 6–7 minutes, then drain immediately. Do not overcook! This may be done ahead.

Melt the butter in a frying pan. Add the cucumbers, salt, pepper, and parsley. Lightly stir-fry just until heated and coated with the butter and parsley. This will serve 4.

Fried Zucchini

In California, fried zucchini is offered as a sports snack at stadiums and home football TV parties, brought with the main course in restaurants, and sometimes just served as a simple accompaniment to a pre-dinner glass of wine. Done right, it can be wonderful. The secret is in the batter.

The Italians created "pastella," the perfect batter for this. It is a simple flour and water mixture that may also be used for frying any other vegetables.

Wash the zucchini and cut into lengthwise sticks. They will look like French fries, or if you wish, they can be a little larger.

1 lb medium sized zucchini
1 cup water
2/3 cup flour
salt and pepper to taste
olive oil or vegetable oil for frying
grated Parmesan cheese (optional)

Pour the water in a bowl. Blend in the flour, stirring until you have a smooth mixture. Add salt and pepper. Pat the zucchini slices dry.

In a frying pan, heat the oil. The amount required will depend on the size of the frying pan. Usually a depth of 1/2" to 3/4" is enough for this shallow frying. Dip the zucchini in the batter and fry in the oil until golden brown on both sides. Sprinkle with Parmesan cheese if desired. Drain on paper towels and serve immediately. This will serve 4.

Easy Artichokes

Artichokes, which need sea breezes to mature, grow on narrow strips of land near the California coast. The fields are incredibly beautiful. The plants have large pale gray-green leaves framing their buds. The small town of Castroville in Monterey County is the heart of artichoke country. Roadside stands sell fresh artichokes from baby size to colossal, along with various bottled marinated artichoke combinations. Locally, rustic and informal restaurants offer artichokes prepared in interesting and creative ways.

Cookbooks offer many recipes for doing complicated things with artichokes. These recipes are a lot of work. The best method for cooking artichokes is still the simplest one. The flavor is not masked and it is fun to slowly savor each leaf, which is really a flower petal!

When you select artichokes, always purchase tightly formed heads. If the leaves are

4 artichokes, medium to large
juice from one lemon
salt and pepper to taste
1-2 cloves of garlic, chopped
1 T. olive oil
mayonnaise or melted butter, for
  dipping

pulling away from the center, the artichoke is getting old.

Cut the stem an inch from the base. If you wish, you may also cut off the thorny top of the artichoke—using a sharp knife, cut straight across the artichoke, an inch down from the top. This is optional.

Heat a large pot of lightly salted water. Add the lemon juice, garlic, salt, pepper, and olive oil. The oil will give a lovely gloss to the leaves. The lemon preserves the green color. Place the artichokes in the pot. Cover and simmer for 45 minutes to one hour. The stem should be tender when pricked with a fork. Remove artichokes and place them on a plate, stem up, to drain. Serve each on a separate plate with a little bowl of mayonnaise or melted butter to "dunk" into. Artichokes are basically finger food. Each leaf is pulled off, one at a time, and dunked in the sauce. The leaf is then drawn through your front teeth, to scrape off the edible inner part of the leaf. The eaten leaves are discarded and dumped in a separate bowl.

Eventually you get to the heart. Scrape the little fuzz away, and dip the heart and stem in the sauce. The heart is the essence of artichoke flavor. One artichoke is served per person. Artichokes may be served either warm or cool.

Refried Beans

Early accounts of California rancho life always mention the abundant use of beans. There was never a meal without beans. Today beans are still popular in California kitchens, especially as an accompaniment to Mexican foods. Creative cooks make spicy hot dips and dab the beans on warmed tortillas with chilies for appetizers. Refried beans are versatile and healthy. The best are the ones you make at home, and this is not a difficult process.

Covered beans with water and soak overnight. Remove any shriveled beans. Drain and place in a large pot covered by water (7–8 cups). Add remaining ingredients, except salt. Cover and simmer, stirring now and then with a wooden spoon, until beans are soft, but not falling apart—about an hour. Stir in salt to taste during the last few minutes of cooking. Salt added at the beginning of the cooking will make your beans tough. Cool and refrigerate overnight

1 lb pink or pinto beans
7–8 cups of water
1 medium onion, diced
2 cloves of garlic, minced
2 tsp. chili powder
1 T. cumin
salt—add at end of cooking

for flavors to mellow. You may, of course, eat the beans now without refrying them. Serve them with a little bean liquid, topped with grated cheddar or Jack cheese.

To make refried beans, measure out about 3/4 cup of cooked beans per person. To make four servings, melt 3 T. bacon drippings or lard in a frying pan—vegetable oil may be used but is not traditional. Add the beans, with a little liquid. Mash the beans with a fork or potato masher as they cook. You want a little texture, not a slick smooth paste. Top with grated jack or cheddar cheese before serving. The favored pan for frying beans is cast iron.

St. Patrick's Day Classic Colcannon

Colcannon is a beautiful blending of fluffy mashed potatoes mingled with cabbage or kale and onions. Homey and humble, it is a fine main dish for a light supper. For heartier fare, add a broiled lamb chop and a pint of Guinness. This will serve 4.

Place the mashed potatoes in a heavy saucepan over low heat. Blend in cabbage or kale and onions. Season to taste with salt and pepper. Keep the colcannon warm in a 300° oven while you prepare the rest of your dinner.

To serve, place a portion on each plate, making a little "well" in the center. Pour the melted butter in the well. Traditionally, colcannon is best eaten with a spoon from the outside in, dipping each spoonful in the butter before popping it in your mouth.

> 4 cups hot mashed potatoes
> 2 cups cooked and drained chopped cabbage or kale
> 4 whole green onions, finely chopped
> 1/2 cup melted butter (1 4-oz. cube)
> salt and pepper to taste

Did you ever eat colcannon when 'twas made with yellow cream,
and the kale and praties blended like the picture in a dream?
Did you ever take a forkful and dip it in the lake
of the clover-flavored butter your mother used to make?
— old Irish song

California Ratatouille

Ratatouille is a classic French Provençal summertime dish. This is the season when vegetables ripen to full flavor in the hot sun.

Ratatouille may be served as a main dish for supper or lunch. Sometime it is used as an accompaniment for roast chicken or pork. In California, where there is always an abundance of fresh produce, this dish is very popular can be found on many restaurant menus.

Cut the zucchini in 1/4-inch slices. Cut each slice in half. Peel the eggplant and cut in 1-inch cubes. Place the zucchini and eggplant in a bowl, sprinkle with salt and let stand 20 minutes to extract excess moisture. Wipe dry and sprinkle with flour.

Heat the oil in a skillet. Cook the onion and garlic just until limp and transparent. Add eggplant, zucchini, bell peppers, salt, and pepper. Cook, covered, over a very low flame, giving a stir every now and then, for 30 minutes.

2 medium zucchini
1 medium eggplant
1/2 cup olive oil
3 T. flour
1 large onion, sliced
2 cloves garlic, peeled and minced
salt and pepper to taste
2 green, yellow, or red bell peppers, seeded and cut in strips
5 ripe tomatoes, peeled and sliced
1 T. capers (optional)
fresh basil leaves for garnish

Remove the cover, lay the tomatoes on top and cook an additional 10 minutes, uncovered. Sprinkle capers on top. Garnish with a few fresh basil leaves. Serve warm, at room temperature, or cold. A friend once served me ratatouille slightly warm, with a light grating of Swiss cheese, and a glass of chilled Provence wine.

Ratatouille will keep in the refrigerator for a week.

Alice Waters' Red Potato and Red Onion Gratin

2 lb red potatoes, about equal size
3 medium red onions
1/4 cup plus 2 T. light olive oil
2–3 sprigs thyme
salt and pepper
2 T. unsalted butter

Part of Alice Waters' talent lies in her ability to use the idea behind a classical French recipe and transform it into a unique dish with a California feeling. This recipe is just the perfect combination of all the ingredients that make up a winning gratin. (Gratin, by the way, does not necessarily refer to a cheese topping, although that is how it is most often thought of in America!) While this gratin is an ideal accompaniment to any main dish, it is equally delicious as a light supper or luncheon dish. This is a favorite of mine.

Peel the potatoes and slice them 1/4-inch thick into a bowl with plenty of cold water. Keep them covered by one inch of water, changing the water as it becomes starchy. The number of changes depends on the potatoes; three to four times is usual.

Peel the onions and slice them 1/4-inch thick. Cook them in 3 T. olive oil with 2 to 3 sprigs of thyme, over very low heat. Cover the pan, but stir occasionally. The onions should be sweet, slightly softened, and, because of the steam effect of keeping the pan covered, still crunchy after 10 minutes. Remove from heat, uncover, and set aside.

Rinse the potatoes in a colander and pat them very dry between tea towels. Toss them in the remaining olive oil.

Layer a lightly oiled shallow 2–3 quart earthenware casserole with potatoes, slightly overlapping them in concentric circles, and salt and pepper lightly. Remove the thyme from the onions, and discard it. Strew some of the onions lightly over the layer of potatoes. Continue layering the onions and potatoes, ending with a layer of potatoes.

Dot with 3 T. softened butter. Bake in a preheated 425° oven for 25 to 30 minutes, until the potatoes are a deep golden brown.

This will serve 6.

145

Salads

Stars of the California Kitchen

Californians have a passion for salad, and often complain when traveling that they miss their salads. It is certainly true that salads are almost a way of life in California. They are used with endless variations for complete meals. California cooks feel a special sense of creativity when they toss and mix their salads.

In our state, the inventive imagination with salads is incredible. Cobb salad, Palace Hotel Green Goddess, and Seafood Louis are all California creations. Presentations can be full of surprises. A salad might be served in melon baskets. Pineapples are hollowed out to serve as salad holders. Lettuce leaves are laid out like a fan for a pretty salad to rest on. The centers of large tomatoes are removed and the interiors filled with marvelous combinations. Salads are garnished with fresh edible flowers and other whimsical delights.

Perhaps one reason salads are so popular is that California supplies nearly 80% of the nation's salad ingredients. Supermarkets and farmers' markets are brimming with tempting choices.

Whether a salad should be served before or after a meal has long been a controversial subject, but the current thought is to simply do what you like. Fortunately the days of heavy iced salads and chilled forks are past, although salads are at their best cool. Remember, salads are fun, healthy, pretty, and adaptable to your own creative ideas.

California Style Niçoise Salad

Niçoise salad originated in the French Riviera city of Nice. It is what is called a "composed" salad—you should have the ingredients all ready and compose them in a pretty arrangement. California cooks like to be creative and add or subtract this or that depending on their moods. This is a basic recipe that reflects current trends.

Optional California ingredients might include 1-1/2 to 2 cups of fresh poached firm fish (tuna, swordfish, etc.) or cooked medium sized shrimp. Peeled orange or tangerine segments (1-1/2 to 2 cups) are also sometimes added. It's fun to include things you enjoy.

To make the dressing, combine the oil, vinegar, mustard, salt, and pepper. Whisk together with a fork.

To make the potato salad, cook six medium white rose potatoes in salted water until tender. Drain, peel, and cut in small cubes. Mix with 1/2 cup of the dressing and refrigerate.

*3 cups French-style potato salad
   (recipe below)*

1-1/2 cups cooked string beans

3 hard-boiled eggs, quartered

4 ripe tomatoes, quartered

12 pitted black olives

*1 green or red pepper, seeded and cut
   in strips*

3 anchovy filets

2 T. capers

2/3 cup olive oil

1/3 cup red wine vinegar

1 tsp. Dijon-style mustard

salt and pepper to taste

lettuce leaves

To compose the salad, arrange the lettuce leaves on a platter. Place the potato salad in the center. Arrange remaining ingredients around the potatoes. The anchovies are cut in narrow strips and laid over the salad in little criss-cross designs. Dot the capers over everything. Drizzle remaining dressing over tomatoes, eggs, string beans, and optional ingredients. This will serve 6 and is perfect for a hot summer evening, served with hot French bread and a chilled rosé wine.

Classic Cobb Salad

Cobb salad is one of our California classics. One evening in 1936, Robert Cobb, president of the famed Brown Derby restaurant, came home late from work. He was hungry, and wondered what to make. Checking the shelves of his refrigerator, Mr. Cobb decided it would be fun to put some things together to make an interesting salad. It came out so well that the next day he tried making it again at the restaurant. His old friend Sid Grauman came in for lunch and was willing to try the new salad. Sid thought it was really terrific, and so it was added to the Brown Derby's menu.

Cobb salad is the perfect dinner for a hot summer day, or for a special occasion such as a wedding shower. Don't let the rather long list of ingredients scare you—once you have made it, you'll see that it is really very easy to create.

Wash the lettuce, discarding any bruised or "tired" leaves. Wash the watercress, using only the top leaves. Wrap the lettuce and

1/2 head iceberg lettuce
1/2 head chicory or endive lettuce
1/2 head romaine lettuce
1/2 bunch of watercress
2 T. minced green onions or chives
2 ripe tomatoes, peeled and seeded
6 slices bacon, cooked crisp and crumbled
3 hard boiled eggs, peeled and chopped
1 ripe avocado, peeled and diced
2 boneless chicken breasts, cooked
lemon juice
2 oz. blue or Roquefort cheese, crumbled

cress in a damp towel, place in a plastic bag, and refrigerate.

Dice the chicken breasts. Squeeze a little lemon juice over them, and refrigerate.

When you are ready to assemble the salad, cut the greens very fine and place in a large bowl or platter. Place the diced chicken over the greens, followed by the green onions.

149

Next add the tomato. Sprinkle the bacon in a strip along the right of the chicken, and the eggs in a strip along the left. Place the avocado around the edges of the dish. Add the blue cheese wherever you think it might look pretty. Making this salad is rather like painting a picture.

Bring the bowl to the table, and pour dressing all over the salad. Usually French dressing is used. You may use bottled, or make your own by combining 1/2 cup salad oil, 3 T. red wine vinegar, 2 T. lemon juice, salt and pepper to taste, and a pinch of dry mustard.

Now, the fun step is to mix all the pretty strips and things all together in a big scramble, combining everything in the bowl. Always mix the salad at the last minute in front of the diners for a sort of dramatic effect. This will serve 4 to 5.

Sunset Papaya Salad

California sunsets can be dramatic, especially along the coast. Often you will see couples holding hands, standing by the surf to watch the last rays of light fade into the Pacific. Sunsets are romantic, and a papaya salad captures that sense in an edible way.

1-1/2 cups red leaf or butter lettuce, washed

1 medium sized papaya, chilled

1/2 cup salted peanuts or roasted macadamia nuts, coarsely chopped

3 T. peanut or salad oil

2 T. rice vinegar

salt and pepper to taste

Tear the lettuce into bite-sized pieces. Peel the papaya, remove the seeds, and cut into small cubes. Blend the oil, vinegar, salt, and pepper. Place the papaya and lettuce in a bowl. Pour the dressing over and mix lightly. Sprinkle the nuts over the salad. Serve at once to 4.

Picnic Pasta Salad

Versatile and healthful, pasta salads are riding a wave of unprecedented popularity. Many creative touches can be added to a basic salad recipe to make a terrific main salad dish. This one is best made a day ahead so the flavors can mellow.

Choose one of the many available pasta shapes, such as little macaroni, green spaghetti, bowls, etc. Cook the pasta per package directions, drain, and rinse with cold water.

In a salad bowl, combine olive oil, vinegar, mayonnaise, salt, pepper, onions, and chopped bell pepper. Add pasta while still warm and mix well. Add any optional ingredients you choose, mix well and chill. Serve garnished with a sprinkling of Parmesan cheese and minced parsley. This will serve 4.

1/2 lb uncooked pasta, such as shells

3 T. olive oil

2 T. red or white vinegar

1/2 cup mayonnaise

salt and pepper to taste

2 minced green onions

1 chopped red or green bell pepper

options: tuna chunks, chicken pieces, slivered ham, peas, cold beef strips, cheese cubes, olives, etc.

Parmesan cheese and minced parsley for garnish

Fresh Mushroom Salad

1 lb fresh mushrooms, lightly washed
1/3 cup olive oil
2 T. fresh lemon juice
salt and pepper to taste
1 T. snipped parsley

In California, no meal is complete without a salad. The varieties are many, and among them is this lovely fresh mushroom salad. Mushrooms are low in calories and contain certain minerals we all need in our diets. Along with being healthy, mushrooms are pretty and fun to eat.

When you shop for mushrooms, always look for ones that are firm and have the cap closed against the stem (as a mushroom gets older, the cap will open away from the stem). Please don't be so obsessive about "dirt" that you soak the mushrooms to clean them— they only need to be quickly whisked under water and wiped with a damp paper towel to remove any tiny dirt crumbs. Remember, mushrooms are grown in a special compost mixture in caves, so you don't need to worry about insects.

Trim the mushrooms by cutting a thin slice off the bottom of each stem. Slice the mushrooms crossways in thin slices, and place in a pretty bowl. Combine remaining ingredients, stir well, and mix with the mushrooms. Refrigerate until serving time. This will serve 4.

Petaluma Victorian Chicken Salad

Petaluma, a Northern California river town, has been many things through its history. The area was a favored home of the gentle Coast Miwok Indians. Later, General Mariano Vallejo, commander of the San Francisco presidio for the Mexican government, settled the valley and built an adobe home with vast ranch lands.

When California became a state, Petaluma developed as a river shipping town serving the rich farmlands. It even had a brief gold rush. Then it became a center for chicken farming.

Through the years, those who became wealthy built lovely Victorian-style houses. Eventually these homes were threatened by sprawling growth that seemed likely to turn the town into ugly, tacky housing for the bay area. The citizens of Petaluma wanted to preserve their past, and voted to maintain this lovely town by only allowing 500 new units to be built each year. Tourists come now to see the historic buildings and enjoy dining along the river.

1 T. butter
2 tsp. curry powder
1/4 cup sherry
4 cups cooked boneless chicken breasts
3/4 cup mayonnaise
2 green onions, minced
salt and pepper to taste
parsley or watercress for garnish

While the chicken industry has moved, leaving only a few farms, Petaluma chickens are still grown for special restaurants and are some of the finest poultry in California. This salad has a Victorian piquancy and is delicious.

Melt the butter in a small pan. Add the curry powder, stir and cook for a minute. Add the sherry and blend in. Remove from stove and cool slightly.

Cut the chicken into bite-sized pieces and place in a salad bowl. Add the curry-sherry mixture, mayonnaise, green onions, salt, and pepper, and mix well with the chicken. Chill until serving time. Garnish with a few sprigs of parsley or watercress, and serve to 4.

Classic San Francisco Crab Louis

Crab Louis is certainly the all-time favorite salad of San Francisco. No one is sure about its true origin. Was it created by the famed Chef Louis from the Poodle Dog, or Solari's, or maybe some other Chef Louis?

The important thing for this salad is that the crab should be very fresh and sweet. San Francisco has over six months of Dungeness crab season, and this is the favored crab to use in this classic dish. Garnishes will vary from cook to cook. I myself prefer none at all; just the delectable crab, dribbled with Louis dressing, on crisp, pale-green iceberg lettuce.

Mix the dressing ingredients together, and refrigerate for an hour or so for the flavors to mingle. In four individual bowls, arrange large lettuce leaves to make a sort of cup shape. Finely shred about 2 cups of the lettuce and place evenly in lettuce cups. Place equal amounts of the crab on the lettuce and cover with dressing.

Louis Dressing

1 cup mayonnaise
1/4 cup whipping cream
1/4 cup chili sauce
3 T. finely minced green onion tops
2 T. finely minced green bell pepper
pinch of cayenne
1 T. lemon juice
salt and pepper to taste

Salad Ingredients

iceberg lettuce
2 cups fresh crab (cooked shrimp or lobster may also be used)

Optional garnishes include black or green olives, tomato wedges, hardboiled egg quarters, or avocado slices. Sourdough bread and a Sauvignon Blanc wine are the perfect accompaniment for this salad. If you are especially hungry for crab, you may want to use this for only 2 servings instead of 4!

154

Bombay Rice Salad

Who is to really know how California salads are given these exotic names from far away places? I have a collection of early California cookbooks and they all include colorful names for recipes. Maybe it is because the state is a melting pot and ethnic influences in our foods are readily accepted and quickly fused into the cuisine of the state. Bombay rice salad is simple to prepare and always popular.

> 3 cups cooked rice (1 cup uncooked)
> 1/2 cup raisins
> 1/2 cup chopped celery
> 1/2 cup mayonnaise or plain yogurt
> 1 tsp. curry powder
> 1 tsp. salt
> 1/2 cup chopped peanuts for garnish

Combine the cooked rice with all the ingredients (except the nuts) while the rice is slightly warm; this helps it to absorb the flavors. Refrigerate, and when ready to serve, garnish with peanuts. This salad is at its best served just slightly cool, not overchilled. The recipe makes 4 good-sized servings.

Tropical Chicken Salad

This salad, with its refreshing tropical flavors, is perfect for hot summer days. It is also a perfect choice for a shower or ladies' luncheon. You can easily prepare this a day ahead. Banana bread is a nice accompaniment for this lovely salad.

> 2 cups cooked and diced chicken breast
> 1 can (8-1/4 oz.) pineapple chunks, or 1 cup fresh pineapple chunks
> 1 cup trimmed celery, cut in small dice
> 1/4 cup macadamia nuts or peanuts, coarsely chopped
> 1 tsp. curry powder
> salt and pepper to taste
> 1/4 cup mayonnaise

Combine all the ingredients in a bowl. Mix together and refrigerate. Garnish with a few fresh cilantro leaves, if desired. This salad will serve 4.

Old Time Spinach Salad

This is the spinach salad of my childhood. It is still my favorite, even though many new fancy, health-obsessional versions are now to be found on restaurant menus. What makes this salad so timeless and good is the way the ingredients all complement each other. It is a very attractive salad, with the white and golden flecks of eggs against the green spinach leaves.

Remove the stems and roots from the spinach leaves. Wash well. Drain and lightly pat dry with a towel. Tear the leaves into

1 bunch of fresh spinach

1 hard-boiled egg, chopped

1/3 cup olive oil or salad oil

3 T. red wine vinegar

1 clove of fresh garlic, minced

4 slices of bacon, fried, drained, and crumbled

salt and pepper to taste

bite-sized pieces, and chill in a plastic bag or dish towel. Just before serving, mix the oil, wine vinegar, salt, and pepper in a salad bowl. Add spinach and toss until coated. Next add the bacon and egg, and give another light toss to blend. This will serve 4.

Variations on a Waldorf Salad

My mother often made this salad, which was a favorite of our family. Then somehow it seemed to be lost and forgotten for a couple of decades, as cold and crispy green salads took the spotlight. Now Waldorf salad has suddenly reappeared, gracing upscale and trendy restaurant menus. New variations have been created that are quite tasty. Waldorf salad makes a refreshing dinner for a summer evening.

Dice the apples, and sprinkle with lemon juice. Add the remaining ingredients and mix gently. Serve on the lettuce leaves. This will serve 4.

3 apples (red, green, or yellow), unpeeled
3 T. lemon juice
1 cup diced celery
1/2 cup coarsely chopped walnuts (can be toasted)
1/2 cup mayonnaise
butter or iceberg lettuce leaves, washed

VARIATIONS: Any of the following may be added: 1 cup cubed chicken, ham, sliced beef, or baby shrimp. For a Mideast flavor, add 1 tsp. curry powder and 1/2 cup raisins. For a Pacific touch, pineapple chunks can be added. Pears used along with the apples are refreshing. Use your imagination and have fun re-creating this American classic.

Mother's Thanksgiving Jello™ Fruit Salad

It is certain that Jello™ fruit salad was not served at the Pilgrims' first Thanksgiving. My mother, however, always made this refreshing salad for Thanksgiving. It may be a little old-fashioned but all our family adores it. Certainly there is something very appealing about fruit shimmering in a cool lemon-flavored gelatin. This salad may be made several days ahead, which will certainly help with Thanksgiving duties. It may be doubled or tripled for larger gatherings.

Mix fruits with lemon juice. Leave some of the red peel on the apples for color. Prepare Jello™ as per package directions, using the pineapple juice (or other juice) as part of the liquid.

1 3-oz. pkg. lemon Jello™

2 cups liquid (fruit juice or water)

2 ripe bananas, diced

2 red Delicious apples, diced

1 8-oz. can of crushed or diced pineapple, drained (use juice as part of the liquid)

2 T. fresh lemon juice

Mix the fruit and Jello™ and place in a pretty mold. Sometimes my mother would add a few peeled and seeded grapes.

This salad may be served as is, or with a dressing made with equal parts of mayonnaise and sour cream, a dash of lemon juice and some slivered toasted walnuts or almonds. This will serve 6.

Lombardy Cauliflower Salad

Cauliflower grows abundantly in California's fertile valleys. Always a popular vegetable, it is a delicious salad ingredient. This recipe came from an Italian family in San Francisco's North Beach area.

When buying cauliflower, always look for firm white heads. When you eat cauliflower, you are actually eating the flower of the vegetable!

Wash and cut the cauliflower into flowerets, that is, bite-sized pieces. Cover with salted

1 large fresh cauliflower, or 2 10-oz. pkgs. frozen
1/4 cup fresh lemon juice
4 T. olive oil
1 whole green onion, minced
1 T. capers
10 pitted black olives, cut in half
salt and pepper to taste

water and cook, covered, for 5 minutes. Mix lemon juice, capers, green onion, and oil in a salad bowl. Place the cauliflower in the bowl and mix, adding salt and pepper to your taste. Garnish with olives and serve. This salad is best served slightly warm. It will serve 3–4.

Mexican Christmas Eve Salad

Mexican families in California have a Christmas tradition that includes a late Christmas Eve supper after mass. This colorful salad is often part of the menu. The use of this dish does not have to be limited to Christmas Eve; it may be served on any happy occasion.

Arrange lettuce in a shallow bowl or platter. Arrange the fruits and beets on the bed of lettuce. Sprinkle with the nuts and pomegranate seeds. Mix oil, vinegar, salt, pepper, and lime juice (if used). Just before serving, pour over the salad and mix gently. This will serve 6.

1 medium sized head of iceberg lettuce

3 oranges, peeled and thinly sliced

2 bananas, peeled and sliced

2 red-skinned apples, cored and thinly sliced

1 cup pineapple chunks

1 cup sliced beets

1 cup chopped peanuts

seeds from 1 pomegranate

1/2 cup salad oil

1/4 cup red wine vinegar

juice from one lime (optional)

salt and pepper to taste

Provençal-California Onion Salad

People from other states often call Californians "rabbits" because we are green salad freaks and eat so much lettuce. Every now and then, we need a break from this lettuce routine. This onion salad of Provençal origin has long been served by vintners in the Napa valley with their barbecue dinners. It is traditionally served slightly warm or at room temperature.

Place the unpeeled onions in an oven-proof dish. Mix the wine and olive oil, and pour over the onions. Bake uncovered at 350° for one hour. If the liquid should dry out during the baking, add a little more oil and wine.

After baking, allow the onions to cool just enough to handle. Peel the onions and slice the best you can—baked onions are a little

6 medium onions, unpeeled, any variety (red and white make a nice combination)
4 T. white wine
2 T. olive oil

Dressing

4 T. olive oil
3 T. red or white wine vinegar
1 tsp. oregano, dried or fresh
salt and pepper to taste
parsley for garnish

tricky to slice perfectly. Place the onions in a pretty bowl. Pour the dressing over them.

Mix the dressing, using a fork, then blend with the sliced onions. Garnish with some snipped fresh parsley. This will serve 4.

Papaya-Avocado Salad with Papaya Seed Dressing

There are a myriad of cooking classes available in California. Even though I teach cooking, there is always something new to be learned from each new class experience. Once I went to a class about papayas. The instructor was in love with papayas. She demonstrated how every part of a papaya can be used. The peeled skin can be rubbed on your face. It will feel cool and give your pores Vitamin A. The flesh can tenderize meat. The seeds may be dried and used as a light pepper. With today's speedy transportation, papayas are available everywhere. To prepare the seeds for use as pepper, just spread them on a plate to dry, then grind in a mill or smash them with a meat tenderizer.

The light green and orange colors make this salad for 4 a most attractive dish. The salad can be made heartier if you wish, by simply adding cooked shrimp, chicken, or crab. A little watercress may also be included in the salad.

1 ripe papaya
2 ripe avocados
butter lettuce

Papaya Seed Dressing

1/2 tsp. dry mustard
1/4 cup sugar
1 tsp. salt
1 cup salad oil
1/2 cup white wine or rice vinegar
1 T. fresh lime or lemon juice
2–3 T. white, red, or green onion, chopped
1 T. papaya seeds

Peel and slice the papaya and avocado. Arrange on top of the lettuce leaves on four plates.

Put all the dressing ingredients, except the papaya seeds, in a blender. Blend to mix. Add the seeds and continue blending just until they are the size of coarse ground pepper. Spoon over the salads to serve. This will make a little over two cups of dressing, so you should have some left over for another salad—this dressing is lovely with fruit salads.

162

Chicken Stroganoff Salad with Walnuts

2 cups egg noodles (dry)
2 cups fresh chopped mushrooms
3 T. butter
3 cups boneless cooked diced chicken
   (any part may be used)
4 whole green onions, minced
1/2 cup mayonnaise
1 cup sour cream
3 T. fresh lemon juice
salt and pepper to taste
1 cup chopped lightly toasted walnuts

Over the last century, California has often been fascinated by Russian ballet stars. They become the toast of the town, and are fêted with parties, press conferences, and television interviews. Once we had a Russian-inspired picnic before a ballet performance, and I invented this salad with Russian flavors.

Cook the noodles in salted boiling water until just tender, and drain. Melt the butter in a frying pan. Lightly brown the mushrooms, and add (with any pan juices) to the noodles. Stir in the chicken and green onions. Blend mayonnaise, sour cream, lemon juice, salt, and pepper together. Mix into salad. Refrigerate until needed. Just before serving, garnish with the walnuts. This will make 6 servings.

Palace Hotel Green Goddess Salad

The Palace Hotel in San Francisco has been one of the world's grand hotels ever since its gala opening in 1875. It has always had a distinguished cuisine, creating extraordinary and unique dishes for San Francisco events.

In 1915, the actor George Arliss was a resident at the Palace while he was appearing in the William Archer play, *Green Goddess*. The chef created a special salad for the opening night dinner. The dressing became the rage of San Francisco, and has remained very popular.

Mix all the ingredients except the lettuce in a one-quart jar or container. Stir or shake to

2 minced green onions

2 T. minced parsley

1 T. fresh tarragon, minced (or 1 tsp dried)

1 T. lemon juice

3 anchovy filets, chopped finely

1-1/2 cups mayonnaise

6–8 cups bite-sized pieces of lettuce (Romaine, red leaf, butter, etc.), washed and chilled

blend well. Chill for several hours or overnight.

To serve, place the greens in a salad bowl. Pour on the dressing and mix well. Serve at once. This will serve 6 generously. For a main dish salad, just add some cooked chicken, shrimp, or crab.

Shanghai Cucumber Salad

A Chinese friend gave me this recipe, which I have used in my cooking classes and for summer parties. You may have to search a little for black sesame seeds. Usually you can find them in grocery stores in your local Chinatown. They add an exciting color and texture crunch to this refreshing salad.

Peel the cucumbers, leaving just a tiny strip of green peel on each side. Run the tines of a fork down the sides of the cucumber. This makes a pleasant design. Slice the cucum-

2 medium sized cucumbers
1 whole green onion, minced finely
1 tsp. black sesame seeds
2 T. sesame oil
1 T. rice wine vinegar
salt and pepper to taste

bers into 1/4-inch slices and sprinkle them with salt. Set them aside for an hour or so. This removes bitter juices and excess moisture. Pat dry and mix with remaining ingredients. Chill until serving time. You may garnish with a few cilantro leaves or a dash of crushed dry hot red peppers.

French Potato Salad with Beef Strips

Although one might not ordinarily think of Los Angeles as a city influenced by the French, they were actually among the first inhabitants of the city. One of the first hospitals was French. There was a French social club and, of course, French restaurants. Many early Los Angeles cookbooks included sections of French recipes.

This potato salad is often used as a main dish in the summertime. The idea is that you begin with a simple stewed-style "pot roast dinner" and save some extra meat and a little stock for the salad.

2 lb potatoes (white rose or red)
1/2 cup white wine or beef stock
salt and pepper to taste
6 T. olive or peanut oil
2 T. red or white wine vinegar
1 tsp. Dijon mustard
2 T. minced green onion or shallot
1 T. minced parsley
2 cups cold beef, cut in julienne strips

Cook the potatoes in their skins just until tender. Do not overcook. Mix the remaining ingredients in a salad bowl, and whisk around with a fork until blended. As soon as the potatoes are cool enough to handle, peel and cut them in slices about 1/8-inch thick. Gently mix with dressing. This will make 6 servings.

Greek String Bean Salad

In California, fresh string beans are almost always available. Of course, in a pinch, frozen may be used. This salad is beautiful and has a zippy Greek flavor. It can be used in place of a hot vegetable as an accompaniment to meat or poultry dishes.

Cut the ends from the beans and wash. Cook the beans in lightly salted water for 5 minutes. Mix remaining ingredients (except walnuts and cheese) in a bowl and stir together. Drain the beans. Place, while still warm, in the bowl with the dressing. Stir so that the dressing coats the beans. This salad may be served chilled or at room temperature. Just before serving, mix in the nuts and cheese. This will serve 4.

1 lb string beans
3 T. olive oil
1 T. red or white wine vinegar
salt and pepper to taste
1 clove of garlic, minced
1 medium sized red onion, minced
1/2 cup lightly toasted walnuts, chopped
3/4 cup Feta cheese, crumbled

Easy Tomato Aspic

Little shimmering squares of tomato aspic have graced many a plate at ladies' luncheons. Somehow this aspic is always a very pleasant touch. It can be molded into hearts, diamonds, circles, or any desired shape. My friend Fran likes to make her aspic with V8™ vegetable juice instead of going through various lengthy tomato procedures. It is perfect simplicity, and has a nice piquant flavor. You can add various seasonings according to your taste.

Soften the gelatin in 1/2 cup of the V8 juice. Heat remainder of V8™ juice to just simmering. Remove from heat and blend in gelatin. Stir to make sure it is well dissolved. Cool slightly and add desired seasonings. Pour into mold and chill for at least 8 hours. Unmold. This will make 8 medium servings.

2 pkgs. unflavored gelatin

1 24-oz. can of V8™ juice

1/4 cup fresh lemon juice

Choice of seasonings:

1/2 to 1 tsp. of celery seed, powdered cumin, chili powder, or fresh basil leaves; 1/2 to 1 cup avocado slices, or finely diced celery, or red pepper

Sicilian Orange Salad

Sicily and California both have orange groves, and both use the orange in many culinary ways. If you have not used oranges in salads, you will be surprised to find how refreshing and colorful they can be. There are seasons when lettuce is expensive and not in good supply, and these are the times to remember this flavorful salad. Sicilian orange salad is colorful for Christmas or a New Year's buffet.

Combine the oranges, olives and onions in a shallow bowl. Drizzle the olive oil over them, sprinkle with black pepper, and mix together so they are well coated. Cover and

3 oranges (Valencia or navel), peeled and thinly sliced

1 medium onion, red or white, thinly sliced

1/2 cup black olives, sliced

black pepper to taste

3 T. olive oil

1/4 cup shelled walnuts, chopped and lightly toasted

parsley for garnish

chill, or put in a cool place for an hour or so, for flavors to mingle.

To serve, sprinkle the walnuts on top with a little minced parsley. This will make 4–5 servings.

Sunny Greek Salad

Greece and California are both renowned for their sunny climates. A zesty Greek salad is as much at home in California as it is in Greece.

Greek-style olives are available in jars or in local delicatessens. Feta is a soft white sheep or goat cheese. To keep feta moist and fresh, remove it from the package and place it in a bowl filled with lightly salted water to cover. Oregano is a favorite herb in Greece, where it grows wild on the hillsides. The name means "joy of the mountain."

Wash the lettuce, cut finely, and place in a bowl. Peel the cucumber, leaving a few "swatches" of green peel to give it color. Slice thinly and place on top of the lettuce. Sprinkle olives and feta cubes over this. Don't worry if your feta does not make perfect cubes, as this cheese can be crumbly. Cut the tomatoes in thin wedges, peeling them if you have time, and place on top of the salad.

1 medium sized head of lettuce (butter lettuce preferred)
3 fresh ripe medium sized tomatoes
1 cucumber
1/2 cup feta cheese, cut in little cubes
10 Greek-style olives (Kalamatas are a favorite)
5 T. olive oil
2 T. fresh lemon juice
1/2 tsp. oregano
salt and pepper to taste

Mix the oil, lemon juice, salt, pepper, and oregano. Pour over the salad and mix gently, so as to not break up the feta. Serve at once. This will serve 4.

Chicken or Shrimp Variation:

Two cups of cooked cubed chicken breast or 1-1/2 cups of cooked bay shrimp may be added to make this salad into a heartier main dish. Warmed pita bread is delicious served with Greek salad.

Sylvia Sebastiani's Bean and Tuna Salad

It is only a few minutes from the historic Sonoma plaza to the Sebastiani vineyards. The Sebastiani tour is one of the most informative and fun in the Sonoma Valley. This delightful salad from Sylvia Sebastiani is wonderful as a side dish with buffets, summer lunches, or barbecues. It is quick, tasty, and very easy.

> 1 15-oz. can kidney beans
> 1/2 cup red onion, chopped
> 1 6-1/2 oz. can tuna
> 4 T. oil
> 2 T. finely chopped parsley
> 1 clove garlic, minced
> 1 T. wine vinegar
> salt and pepper to taste

Drain and rinse beans in a colander. Mix all the ingredients in a bowl, adding salt and pepper to taste. Chill. This recipe will make 4–6 portions.

Julia Child and Caesar Salad

When I started to work on this California cookbook, there were some recipes that I knew would have to be included. Caesar salad was one of them, because it is a California institution. I have enjoyed many versions of this salad; one of the first was in Tijuana, Mexico, where it originated.

I am a Julia Child fan. We were both born in Pasadena and we both lived in Paris at the same time. I wish I had known her in Paris, but I did not, and only met her in California. I read her cookbooks over and over; they are like lusty novels I cannot put away. When I need some information about a recipe, or other culinary information, I turn to Julia. I remembered reading about her experiences with Caesar salad, and felt she has written about this salad in a mythicizing way that no other Californian could, and so, with her permission, here is Julia's "Musings upon Caesar and his Salad."

(continued on next page)

(continued from previous page)

"One of my early remembrances of restaurant life was going to Tijuana in 1925 or 1926 with my parents, who were wildly excited that they should finally lunch at Caesar's restaurant. Tijuana, just south of the Mexican border from San Diego, was flourishing then, in the prohibition era. People came from the Los Angeles area in droves to eat in the restaurants; they drank forbidden beer and cocktails as they toured the bars of the town; they strolled in the flowered patio of Aqua Caliente listening to the marimba band, and they gambled wickedly at the casino. Word spread about Tijuana and the good life, and about Caesar Cardini's restaurant and about Caesar's salad.

"My parents, of course, ordered the salad. Caesar himself rolled the big cart up to the table, tossed the romaine in a great wooden bowl, and I wish I could say I remember his every move, but I don't. The only thing I can see clearly is the eggs. I could see him break 2 eggs over that romaine and roll them in, the greens going all creamy as the eggs flowed over them. Two eggs in a salad? Two one-minute coddled eggs? and garlic-flavored croutons and grated Parmesan cheese? It was a sensation of a salad from coast to coast, and there were even rumblings of its success in Europe.

"How could a mere salad cause such emotion? But, one remembers that this was way back in 1924, when Caesar Cardini invented it, and it was only in the early twenties that refrigerated transcontinental transportation came into being. Before then, when produce was out of season in the rest of the country, there was no greenery to be had. Before then, too, salads were considered rather exotic, definitely foreign, probably Bolshevist, and anyway, food only for sissies.

"Almost 50 years later, when we decided upon Caesar salad as one of the events for our program "Kids want to cook," I had as usual, studied all the sources and found there was not any agreement among any of them. I evolved what appealed to me, but it lacked a certain authenticity, and it had no drama. Then my producer, Ruthie, suggested we try and locate someone from that era who knew Caesar and really knew the salad. Was there anyone? Indeed there was; Ruthie found that Rosa Cardini, his daughter, was living in the Los Angeles area, and was the head of a successful spice and salad dressing business. I had a long Boston-to-Los Angeles telephone conversation with her, taking copious notes. She was born five years after her father created his masterpiece, she said, but she knew every detail because it had been so much discussed and remembered.

"As we went over each move, the salad began to take on life for me. At first, she said, Caesar used only the tender inside leaves, the hearts, of romaine, and he served them whole, arranging each portion on a large chilled salad plate, leaf by leaf; you picked up a leaf by its stem end, and you ate it in your fingers, leaf by leaf. What a great idea! What fun for television. But, she went on, since most Americans do not like plucking up sauced items with their fingers, he later changed to bite-sized pieces. Was there anything special in the way he manipulated the salad? Yes, he had a uniquely Caesar way of tossing the salad. In fact he didn't toss it, he scooped under the leaves to make them turn like a large wave breaking toward him, to prevent those tender shoots of green from bruising. How about anchovies, mustard, herbs, and so forth? No! No anchovies! Caesar never used anything but the best oil, fresh lemons, salt and pepper, a little Worcestershire—that's where those anchovies crept into so many of the recipes I have seen: Worcestershire does have a speck of anchovy. Caesar insisted on the best and freshest Parmesan, and homemade croutons basted with oil in which fresh garlic has been steeped.

"That is the way we did the salad on our television program, and I have always been delighted with it. It is a simple salad, really, and its beauty rests entirely in the excellence of its ingredients— the best and freshest of everything."

Caesar Salad

The Romaine

You want 6–8 whole unblemished leaves of romaine, between 3 and 7 inches long, per person. Strip the leaves carefully from the stalks, and refrigerate the rejects in a plastic bag, reserving them for another salad. Wash your Caesar leaves gently, to keep them from breaking; shake dry, and roll loosely in clean towels. Refrigerate until serving time.

The Croutons

Puree the garlic in a small heavy bowl, and mash to a smooth paste with a pestle or spoon, adding 1/4 tsp. salt and dribbling in 3 T. of olive oil. Strain into a medium sized frying pan and heat to just warm. Add the croutons, toss for about a minute over moderate heat, and place them into a nice serving bowl.

2 large crisp heads romaine lettuce

2 large cloves garlic

salt

3/4 cup best quality olive oil

2 cups best quality, plain, unseasoned toasted croutons

1 lemon

2 eggs

1/4 cup (1 oz.) genuine, imported Parmesan cheese, freshly grated

peppercorns in a grinder

Worcestershire sauce

Other Preliminaries

Shortly before serving, squeeze the lemon into a pitcher, boil the eggs for exactly 1 minute, grate the cheese into another nice little bowl, and arrange all of these on a tray along with the rest of the olive oil, the croutons, pepper grinder, salt, and Worcestershire. Have large dinner plates chilled, arrange the romaine in the largest salad bowl you can find, and you are ready to go.

Mixing the Salad

Prepare to use large and rather slow and dramatic gestures for everything you do, as though you were Caesar himself. First pour 4 T. of oil over the romaine. Give the leaves 2 rolling tosses—hold salad fork in one hand, spoon in the other, and scoop under the leaves at each side of the bowl, bringing the implements around the edge to meet each other opposite you, then scoop them up toward you in a slow roll, bringing the salad leaves over upon themselves like a large wave breaking toward you; this is to prevent bruising as you season them. Sprinkle on 1/4 tsp. of the salt, 8 grinds of pepper, 2 more spoonfuls of oil, and give another toss. Pour on the lemon juice, 6 drops of Worcestershire, and break in the eggs. Toss twice, sprinkle on the cheese. Toss once, then sprinkle on the croutons, and give 2 final tosses.

Serving

Arrange the salad rapidly but stylishly, leaf by leaf, on each large plate, stems facing outward, and a sprinkling of croutons at the side. Guests may eat the salad with their fingers, in the approved and original Caesar manner, or may use knives and forks—which they will need anyway for the croutons.

Eggs and Brunch

California Mornings

Brunches are one of the most popular ways of entertaining in California. Brunches can be held at any convenient time in the morning. Guests may linger into early afternoon if everyone is having a pleasant time. One reason brunches are such a favorite is because these hours are agreeable for everyone. There is no need to rush anywhere; there will still be time left in the day after brunch for other activities.

In the summer, brunches may be held on flower-decked patios or at shaded tables on green lawns. In the winter, the food may be spread on a kitchen table or perhaps placed in front of a cozy fire. There is always room for creativity in serving.

Many of these recipes can be prepared ahead so the host and hostess may visit with guests. Brunch is a favorite way to relax in California.

Huevos Rancheros

When we go to visit my son Bob in Santa Barbara, we like to drive along the coast instead of taking the hot inland freeway. The road goes through the agricultural town of Oxnard, where many Mexican farm workers live. This means there are some very good Mexican restaurants in this town.

Often we stop for a late breakfast of huevos rancheros. These are eggs cooked in a zesty tomato sauce, served on a tortilla and topped with grated cheese. They are easy to make at home for brunch, and go terrifically well with refried beans and a pitcher of sangria.

Heat the oil or lard in a frying pan. Lightly cook onion and garlic just until limp. Add tomatoes and seasonings. Simmer over a low flame for 15 minutes.

Carefully break the eggs and slip them into the simmering sauce. Cover and poach until eggs are cooked (about 5 minutes). Heat the

2 T. vegetable oil or lard
2 medium onions, chopped
2 cloves of garlic, minced
1 28-oz. can of diced or solid pack tomatoes
1 fresh Anaheim chile, chopped, or 1/4 cup canned diced chiles
1 tsp. cumin
1 tsp. chili powder
pinch of salt
4 eggs
4 corn tortillas
cheddar cheese, grated, for garnish
sliced avocado for garnish (optional)

tortillas by wrapping them in foil and heating for a few minutes in the oven. To serve, place the tortilla on a warm plate. Carefully remove egg and place on the tortilla, circled by the sauce. Top with grated cheese and avocado slices. This will serve 4, or, if you are extra hungry, 2.

Deceitful Cheese Soufflé

This is not a recipe for a classic soufflé, but it looks and tastes a lot like the real thing. It is perfect for a brunch, as everything is made ahead of time, and it only needs to be baked. For California brunches, it is usually served with fresh fruit and champagne.

Remove the crusts, butter the bread slices, and cut them into cubes. Butter a 9″ X 13″ (or close) baking dish. Place half the cubes in the dish. Sprinkle with the cheese. Place the mushrooms, if used, on top of the cheese. Repeat the bread cubes and cheese. Mix remaining ingredients and pour over the bread and cheese.

butter at room temperature for buttering bread

9 large slices of wheat or white bread

1 lb grated cheese (cheddar, Jack, etc.)

1/2 lb fresh mushrooms, cleaned and sliced (optional)

6 eggs, beaten

2 cups half-and-half

2 cups milk

1 T. Dijon-style mustard

Cover with foil or plastic wrap and refrigerate overnight. Bake for 1 hour at 350 degrees. The top should be bubbly and light brown. Cut in squares to serve 8.

San Francisco Spinach Soufflé

I have always loved vegetable soufflés. These pretty, fluffy combinations are to be found on many menus in San Francisco. One of the best is this simple blend of cheese, eggs, and spinach. This recipe is nearly foolproof, and though the result will not be as high and puffy as some magazine food photos, it is delicious for brunch or a lovely lunch.

Melt the butter, stir in the flour, and blend well. Add the milk, stirring slowly. Add the cheese, onion, salt, and pepper as the sauce is cooking. When the sauce is thick and the cheese has melted, mix the egg yolks with a fork and stir into the sauce along with the spinach. It is important that the spinach be well drained.

Beat the egg whites until stiff, fold into the spinach mixture, and place in a well-but-

4 T. flour

4 T. butter

1 cup milk

1 cup grated Jack or cheddar cheese

1 tsp. chopped onion

salt and pepper to taste

1 cup chopped cooked spinach (fresh or frozen), well drained

3 eggs, separated

tered, 2-quart loaf or round baking pan. Place this pan in a larger pan into which you have put enough water to come halfway up the sides of the soufflé pan. This produces a moist soufflé. Bake at 350° for 45 minutes. The soufflé will serve 3 to 4 people. Other vegetables may be substituted for the spinach, but remember that all those things Popeye said about spinach making you strong are really true.

Italian Vegetable-of-your-choice Frittata

It comes as a bit of a surprise, when you are in Italy, to find that such a thing as a big American breakfast is unknown. Dark flavorful cups of espresso and a roll are the usual morning fare. Eggs for breakfast are rare, something for invalids or pregnant ladies. This is not to say Italians do not like eggs, they just use them in different ways. One of their greatest egg creations is the frittata.

The frittata is a way to combine various ingredients in a sort of flat scramble. It might be served as part of a lunch or light dinner, or a single wedge makes a snack or appetizer. When I lived in Italy, I became quite taken with this versatile way of preparing eggs. When I returned to California, I began to use the frittata as a main dish for brunch. The ingredients can be changed according to what is available in the market or your refrigerator. It is a food where one can use imagination and have fun.

Place the eggs, salt, pepper, 1/4 cup of the cheese and the vegetables in a bowl. Mix gently with a fork to combine. Heat the oil

6 fresh eggs

salt and pepper to taste

1/2 cup grated Parmesan cheese (Romano or Jack or other may be used)

1-1/2 cups of cooked and well drained vegetables (zucchini, spinach, eggplant, olives, broccoli, etc.)

4 T. olive oil

2–3 fresh tomatoes for garnish

in a frying pan. Pour in the egg mixture. Cook over a medium flame until you see that the sides are set and firm. Remove from the flame. Sprinkle the remaining 1/4 cup of cheese on the top, and place under a broiler until cheese is browned and the center of the frittata is cooked. Some cooks can flip the frittata over in the pan, but this requires a lot of skill.

Cool slightly. Cut in wedges and serve garnished with tomato slices. If you prefer your tomatoes cooked, add them before broiling. This recipe will serve 3, but can easily be enlarged to serve more.

Gold Miner's Hangtown Fry

California's Highway 49 winds through territory that was settled in the famous gold rush of 1849. This is a beautiful place to visit in the spring. There are dense patches of wildflowers dotted upon fields of green grass, and snow still clings to the peaks of the Sierra Nevada mountains. The area is full of historic markers, cozy bed-and-breakfast inns, and some of the state's oldest wineries.

The tale of "Hangtown fry" is part of the lore of the gold rush. The present city of Placerville was once known as Hangtown because more men were hanged there than in any other city. (The name was changed because today's residents preferred to put all that behind them.)

There are two stories about the origin of this famous California meal, and each has some historic claim to validity. The first is that a local miner was sentenced to be hung for stealing a horse. As it was the custom for a condemned man to be granted a last meal

---

12 large fresh eggs

1 pint small Eastern oysters (if you use Western oysters, cut them in half)

2 additional eggs, beaten, for breading

cracker meal as needed

1/2 cup butter

salt and pepper to taste

watercress for garnish

1 bottle of champagne

---

before the sentence was carried out, he requested oysters fried with eggs, and champagne. While the hangmen went to prepare this, friends of the miner arrived and helped him to escape. The hangman returned with the meal and, as there was not anyone to hang, he sat down and ate this wonderful combination.

According to the second account, a weary and grimy miner walked into the Carey House hotel, tossed some gold nuggets on the table, and demanded the most expensive meal in the hotel. The cook combined some costly eggs and oysters and served them with a bottle of fine French champagne. Eggs cost at least a dollar apiece. Oysters were shipped up the Sacramento river in ice and were also expensive. Champagne from France could be $100 per bottle.

I have always been fascinated with these stories, and I am passionate about this beautiful flavor combination. Many years ago I began a tradition in our family of serving this for holiday breakfasts or brunches. You can prepare sourdough toast to continue the mining theme.

Drain the oysters. Dip each in the egg and then in the cracker meal. This may be done ahead.

Heat 1/4 cup of the butter in a frying pan (nonstick works well). Fry oysters on both sides until golden brown. Season with salt and pepper. Set aside in a warm place.

In another frying pan, melt the remaining 1/4 cup of butter. Mix the eggs with a fork, add salt and pepper to taste, and scramble over a low flame. Fold in oysters at the last moment. Do not overcook. Serve at once on warmed plates to 6, with chilled glasses of champagne. Garnish with watercress sprigs.

Bagels and Lox

Bagels and lox are the answer for a quick, last-minute brunch, and all you need is a trip to your nearest deli. Purchase enough smoked salmon for the expected number of guests. Usually 1 lb will serve 4.

Two bagels are needed per person. Place the salmon on a platter and the bagels in a basket. Serve with a bowl of sour cream and a bowl of sweet butter. Capers and finely chopped onions may be set out as well. In California, the favorite beverage to accompany this is champagne, although sometimes beer is served. Guests help themselves, and make up their own bagels and lox. This menu is fun and very easy.

183

Special French Toast

French toast should not be overlooked as a brunch favorite. It is especially good when made with sturdy sourdough bread, as they do in San Francisco. It can be fried quickly and kept warm in the oven. Serve it with crisp bacon or sausage, and a bowl of sliced fresh oranges.

Mix eggs, milk, and salt together. Place in a shallow pan or bowl. Heat a good amount of oil and butter together in a frying pan. A nonstick pan is useful for French toast.

3 eggs
1 cup milk
1/4 tsp. salt
*an equal mixture of butter and
    vegetable oil for frying*
*8 slices of day-old sourdough
    (or other) bread*

Dip each piece of bread in the egg mixture. Lift out and let excess batter drip back into bowl. Fry on both sides until golden brown. Place cooked slices on a platter in a 200° oven to keep warm as you are frying the bread. This will serve 4. Maple syrup, or sugar and cinnamon make delicious toppings.

Scrambled Eggs Piperade

Piperade is a Basque-inspired combination of red and green peppers, onions, and garlic, lightly fried in olive oil. The colors are attractive and the taste peppy. This zesty vegetable mixture is folded into scrambled eggs for a delicious main dish at brunch.

Heat the olive oil in a frying pan. Add onion and cook over low flame for a few minutes, until limp. Add garlic and peppers and stir-fry for 3–4 minutes.

3 T. olive oil
1 garlic clove, minced
1 medium onion, sliced
1 medium red bell pepper
1 medium green pepper
8 eggs
salt and pepper to taste

Mix eggs lightly with a fork, seasoning with salt and pepper. Add to the piperade mixture and scramble over a low flame until the eggs are cooked. This will serve 4. Sangria is the perfect beverage accompaniment for this.

Scotch Eggs

My first experience with Scotch eggs was at the Museum Tavern on Great Russell Street in London. Staff from the British museum favor this pub, and they enjoy having Scotch eggs with their pints. The eggs looked very appealing to me and I tried them. It was love at the first bite and since then I have been preparing them for picnics, brunches, or as little appetizers. They are a versatile food, and all my California friends wanted the recipe. The secret is to purchase a good quality bulk sausage. Any desired sausage flavor mixture may be used.

Pat the eggs dry with a paper towel. Dust with the flour. Dampen your hands with cool water and take a little handful of sausage.

6 hard-boiled eggs, cooled and shelled
1 lb bulk sausage
1 egg, beaten
bread crumbs or cracker meal
a little flour
1/3 cup cooking oil

Mold a thin "skin" of sausage around each egg. Keeping your hands moist will help this procedure. Dip the prepared eggs in the beaten egg and then in the crumbs or meal. Heat the oil in a frying pan (nonstick works well). Brown the eggs on all sides, rolling them around as they cook. Scotch eggs are served cut in half, chilled, on a lettuce leaf. They may also be served hot, right out of the pan, for brunch or a light supper.

Hermosa Beach Chili Rellenos

I am addicted to chili rellenos. Whenever I am on a vacation, after about a week I begin dreaming of chili rellenos. The zesty green chiles filled with melted cheese deliver delight with every bite. Once I was confined to the Jules Stein Hospital at UCLA, due to an eye operation. The food was dreadful and although my eye was recovering well, I thought I might end up with malnutrition. I complained to my friends, and one day at lunch they popped into my room with a take-out foil pan filled with chili rellenos from my favorite Mexican restaurant. I was saved, and immediately felt marvelous. Green chilies are, after all, full of Vitamin C and other healthy things.

The first thing I do when I return home from any vacation is to make a chili relleno dinner. At first I had problems getting the batter to stick to the chilies. Most recipes tell you to dip the chilies in the batter, but on the way to the frying pan it all runs off the slippery chilies and makes a big mess.

6 whole green chilies, fresh or canned
3 eggs, separated
salt and pepper to taste
1/2 lb Jack or cheddar cheese
1/4 cup vegetable oil or lard

After some experimenting I developed this method which is easy and produces a beautiful golden brown relleno.

If you are using fresh chilies: Remove the skins by placing the chilies under the broiler and turning until they are brown on all sides. Carefully slip them into a plastic bag while they are still warm. Immediately cover the bag with a damp dishtowel, and leave it for 15 minutes. This will make the skins easy to remove. Cut a slit down the side of each chili and carefully remove the seeds. Leave the stem on.

Take a long slice of cheese, the size of the chile, and place inside the chili.

Beat the egg whites until stiff. Lightly beat the yolks and fold into the whites. Season with salt and pepper.

(continued on next page)

(continued from previous page)

In a large frying pan (nonstick works well), heat the lard or oil. With a large spoon, place a long dollop of egg batter, the size of the chili, in the hot oil or lard. Now gently place the chili on this "bed" of batter, and dribble some more batter on the top. Flip over to cook golden brown on both sides. Do not crowd in the pan. Serve at once with sour cream and salsa. This will serve 2 as a main dish with some rice and beans.

Stratas for Fun and Easy Brunches

The word "strata," from the Latin, simply means horizontal layers of any material. In the recipe world, stratas are layers of bread, cheese and other tidbits, covered with a seasoned egg mixture and allowed to mellow in the refrigerator. This works out very well for brunch. You prepare the strata the evening before. The next morning just pop it in the oven before your guests arrive. Serve with fresh sliced fruit, and hot rolls or croissants.

Here are several variations on the strata theme.

Chili Relleno Strata

Place the bread in a shallow baking pan (11″ × 7-1/2″ × 2″ or close), buttered side down. Sprinkle the cheddar over the bread. Next sprinkle the Jack over the cheddar and finish with the chilies.

In a bowl, lightly beat the eggs. Add the milk and seasonings. Blend well and pour over the bread and cheese layers. Cover and refrigerate at least four hours or overnight. Bake uncovered in a 325° oven about 50 minutes. This will serve 6.

6 slices of white bread (day old is best), lightly buttered

1-1/2 cups grated cheddar cheese

1-1/2 cups Jack cheese

1 4-oz. can diced green chilies (or more if you adore chiles)

6 eggs

2 cups milk

1 tsp. oregano leaves

salt and pepper to taste

1 tsp. cumin seed or powdered cumin

1 tsp. chili powder

Becky's Mushroom Strata

My friend Becky is a school teacher and loves to entertain her colleagues, friends, and neighbors. Her strata recipe is especially good for a summer lunch or brunch.

In a frying pan, melt the butter and lightly stir and fry the mushrooms for just a minute. Set aside.

Butter the bread and cut it into cubes. Line the bottom of a lightly buttered 8" × 11" pan (or close) with half the bread cubes. Combine mushrooms, onion, celery, green pepper, mayonnaise, salt, and pepper. Spread half of this mixture over the bread. Top with remaining half of the bread. Spread the rest of the mushroom mixture on the bread. Combine eggs and milk. Pour over strata and refrigerate overnight.

1 lb fresh mushrooms, washed and sliced
8 slices of white bread
1/2 cup minced white onion
1/2 cup celery, diced
1/2 cup green pepper, diced
1/2 cup mayonnaise
salt and pepper to taste
2 eggs
1-1/2 cups milk
1 can cream of mushroom soup
3/4 cup cheddar cheese, grated
4 T. butter, plus some extra for buttering the bread

Spread mushroom soup over strata. Bake at 350° for 40 minutes. Sprinkle cheese over top. Bake an additional 10 minutes. This will serve 6.

Cheese Strata with Olives and Sausage

This strata has a snappy California flavor and is wonderful served with hot buttered tortillas and tomato salsa.

Trim the crusts from the bread and butter one side. Place the bread, buttered side down, in a shallow pan (12″ × 9″ × 2″ or close) and spread the cheese over it. Crumble and brown the sausage, drain, and let cool. Combine eggs, milk, mustard, onions, olives, salt and pepper, and sausage. Pour this mixture over the bread and cheese. Cover and refrigerate at least four hours or overnight.

10 slices of white bread (day old), buttered, 4–5″ square

3 cups of grated cheddar cheese (about 3/4 lb)

1/2 lb bulk sausage, any desired style

4 eggs, beaten

3 cups milk

1 tsp. Dijon mustard

2 whole green onions, minced

1 cup chopped olives

salt and pepper to taste

Bake at 325° for 45–50 minutes. The top should be browned and puffy. Let stand a few minutes before cutting into squares. This will serve 6.

Joe's Special

Joe's Special was improvised late one evening at the New Joe's Restaurant in San Francisco. Some hungry customers came in and wanted something to eat immediately. All that remained in the refrigerator at the end of a busy day were eggs, spinach, and hamburger. The resourceful cook combined these ingredients and created this San Francisco classic.

It is a terrific breakfast dish that can be made in very little time.

In a frying pan, heat the butter and oil. Add the hamburger and onions, and cook over a medium flame until the meat is browned. Add the spinach and seasonings. Cook together for a minute. Stir in the eggs and cook, stirring, just until the eggs are set. Do not overcook. This will make 4 servings, or 2 if you are very hungry. Hash browns are usually served with Joe's Special. Garnish each plate with some wedges of fresh tomato if you want to add some color.

1 lb lean ground beef

1 T. olive oil and 1 T. butter

3 chopped green onions, or 1/2 medium onion, chopped

1 cup cooked spinach, fresh or frozen, well drained

salt and pepper to taste

4 eggs, slightly beaten

1 pinch of basil or oregano (optional)

Optional: 1/4 lb of fresh sliced mushrooms, added to meat while cooking

Toad in the Hole

I first had this simple and wonderful British creation when a friend from England was visiting and offered to prepare it for a light supper. I will admit that I was a little curious about the name, but Jill explained that sausages are called "toads" and the batter is the "hole." It is true that when the dish is cooked, the sausages poke up from the batter in rather peculiar shapes. "Toads" make a good main dish for a brunch. They may be served with freshly baked scones and fresh berries to maintain the English spirit.

Beat the eggs, with salt, until frothy. Slowly add the flour and the milk, alternately. Beat well until the mixture is very smooth. This may be done with a blender, mixer, or by hand. The secret is not to have any lumps. Refrigerate for an hour.

> 2 eggs
> 1 cup all-purpose flour
> 1 cup milk
> salt and pepper to taste
> 1 pound small pork sausages (or any other type of small sausages)

Brown the sausages and dribble 2 T. of their drippings into an 8″ (or close) square baking dish or a 10″ pie pan. Arrange the sausages in the pan. Carefully pour the batter over them. Bake in a pre-heated 400° oven for 30 minutes. Sometimes the British place a pot of mustard on the table for a toad condiment.

Cut in squares so that each portion will have some "toads." This will serve 4 and can easily be increased for a larger party.

Portsmouth Square Eggs Foo Yung

San Francisco's Chinatown is the second largest in the nation. Its restaurants offer food from every region of China. One dish that has always remained popular is this simple and satisfying eggs foo yung. It is easy to prepare at home for a tasty dinner.

Beat the eggs in a bowl until slightly thick. Add the rest of the ingredients, except the oil, and blend. Do not prepare this ahead, as it will get watery. This is a last-minute affair.

Heat the oil in a frying pan. When oil is hot, take a large spoon and pour about 1/4 cup of the batter into the oil. Repeat the procedure until you have as many pancakes as your pan will hold without overcrowding. Cook a few minutes on one side and then turn. Each side should be light brown. You may need an extra turn to get the perfect doneness. This will make about 8 pancakes.

To make the sauce, place the broth in a saucepan and whisk in the cornstarch and soy sauce. Heat slowly while whisking until the sauce is slightly thickened. Dribble this over the egg foo yung.

3 eggs

1 cup fresh bean sprouts

1/4 cup minced pork, chicken, or shrimp (optional)

1 T. soy sauce

2 T. minced green onion

3–4 T. peanut or salad oil

Sauce

1 cup chicken broth

1 T. cornstarch

1 T. soy sauce

Bread, Muffins and Pizza

Who hasn't heard of San Francisco sourdough bread or the eclectic flavor combinations of California pizzas? There are, however, many other lovely bread-related recipes, using local dates, oranges, olives, and honey. Yeast recipes are not included in this chapter, as California cooks often prefer the quick and easy breads.

Tortillas are used as a kind of bread in California. Most people prefer not to make them at home, but tortillas are readily available in markets nationwide, and may easily be frozen.

My first happy bread memory is of my grandpa taking the center out of a hot crusty French roll and dabbing it with sweet butter. He would feed it to me like I was a little bird.

The first bread creation I learned to make was a muffin recipe at Audubon Junior High. Muffins are easy, and Mrs. Armstrong, our happy home economics teacher, taught us all the variations. I was proud of my muffin baking ability, and made muffins for my family every chance I had.

A good loaf of bread, a well-made sandwich, or a tasty pizza are always a joy and fill a special need for all of us.

Cinnamon Raisin Wheat Bread

The scent of cinnamon will fill your kitchen as you bake this easy bread, a favorite for California breakfasts. The slices may be spread with honey, marmalade, or cream cheese, and served with freshly made scrambled eggs.

The bread is all mixed in one bowl and takes only a few minutes to prepare.

Mix buttermilk and egg together. Stir in brown sugar. Sift dry ingredients and stir into egg and buttermilk mixture. Blend in raisins.

1 egg
1 cup buttermilk
1 cup brown sugar
2 cups wheat flour (or 1 cup white and 1 cup wheat)
1 tsp. baking soda
1 T. cinnamon
1 tsp. salt
1-1/2 cups raisins

This can all be stirred with a fork or spoon. You do not need any electric appliance. Place the dough in a greased 9″ × 5″ bread pan and bake at 350° for 45 minutes.

Pacific Ginger Bread

In the past few years, fresh ginger has become increasingly popular in California. This is partly due to the increased population of Asian-Americans, who use ginger abundantly in their cuisine. Fresh ginger is the root of the ginger plant and can be found in the produce section of supermarkets. When you buy it, make sure it is firm and smooth. Only buy what you need, and do not be intimidated by breaking off a small piece. Store it in the refrigerator. This ginger-scented bread is easy to make and perfect for any use.

Combine the buttermilk, grated ginger, oil, egg, lemon rind, and salt. Mix lightly until blended.

Sift the remaining dry ingredients into a bowl. Make a well in the center of this mixture. Pour buttermilk mixture into the well. Stir all together until you have a smooth mixture. Do not overmix.

1 cup buttermilk
3–4 T. peeled, grated fresh ginger root
1/4 cup peanut or vegetable oil
1 egg
grated rind of one lemon
1/2 tsp. salt
2-1/2 cups all-purpose flour
2/3 cup sugar
1 tsp. baking soda
1 tsp. baking powder
1/2 tsp. cinnamon
1/8 tsp. ground cloves

Grease and flour a 9″ × 5″ × 3″ loaf pan. Place the dough in the pan and bake at 350° for 1 hour and 10 minutes. Cool on a wire rack for 5 minutes and remove from pan. This bread is delicious with honey butter (butter at room temperature, mixed with an equal amount of honey) or marmalade butter (the same procedure but with an equal amount of marmalade).

Chili Olive Bread

The combination of olives with a touch of chili adds a California zest to this easy to make bread. It is especially nice with salads or a soup dinner.

In a mixing bowl, beat the eggs with the olive oil until blended. Add the olives, and chilies if used. Sift the dry ingredients and add alternately with the milk to the egg mixture. Mix together just until everything is blended. The dough will be somewhat thick. Grease a bread pan with olive oil. Place bread batter in pan and bake at 350° for one hour. Remove from pan and cool on rack.

2 eggs
2 T. olive oil
1 cup chopped black olives
2 T. diced canned chilies or fresh Anaheim chilies (optional)
2 cups flour
2 tsp. baking powder
1 T. sugar
1 tsp. salt
1 tsp. chili powder
1/2 cup milk

Garlic Bread

Garlic bread goes with everything. It is traditional, simple to prepare, and delicious.

> 1 long loaf of French, sourdough, or
>   Italian bread
> 1/2 cup butter at room temperature
> 2–3 cloves of garlic, minced

Mix together the garlic and butter until blended. Split the bread in half lengthwise. Spread with the garlic butter. Place the loaf together again. Wrap it in foil and bake for 15 minutes in a 450° oven. If you are barbecuing, place the wrapped loaf on the barbecue rack for about 15 minutes, turning once.

Mother's Onion Bread

My mother made this bread with our spaghetti dinners and barbecues. The onion slices mingle deliciously with the butter.

> 1 long loaf of French or sourdough
>   bread
> 1/2 cup butter at room temperature
> 1 onion, any variety, sliced thinly

Lay the bread on a board and cut partially into 3/4″ slices. Do not cut all the way through the loaf; leave about 1/2″ of the bottom crust intact. Butter each slice and place a slice of onion in between slices. Press the loaf together and wrap in foil. Bake at 450° for 15 minutes, or place on rack over barbecue coals for 15 minutes. Turn once during cooking.

Prune Buttermilk Corn Bread

California produces more prunes than any other place in the world, so it is only natural that prunes are used in many of our recipes.

Prunes were brought to Santa Clara in 1856, from France. For the long voyage around the Horn, the cuttings were stuck into raw potatoes, packed in sawdust and placed in leather trunks. Most prunes sold today are tender, pitted, and ready for quick and easy use in cooking.

Sift flour, baking powder, baking soda, and salt into a bowl. Combine eggs, sugar, buttermilk, butter, corn meal, and prunes. Stir to blend all ingredients. Pour the dry mixture into the buttermilk mixture and mix to make a smooth dough. Lightly grease a glass or metal 9" × 12" baking dish. Pour the batter into the pan. Bake at 400° for 25–30 minutes. The sides and top should be browned. Cool the pan on a rack. Cut the bread into squares to serve. This bread will serve 8 and is at its best when slightly warm.

2 cups all-purpose flour
2 tsp. baking powder
1 tsp. baking soda
1/2 tsp. salt
2 eggs
1/2 cup sugar
2 cups buttermilk
1/4 cup melted butter, slightly cooled
1 cup cornmeal
1 cup pitted prunes, cut in small pieces

Honey Bread

Californians generally like desserts that are fresh and simple. This, of course, is not always the rule, and we are sometimes quite self-indulgent. On the whole, however, there is a trend towards fresh ices, frozen yogurt, or tasty cookies served with fresh California fruit. Honey bread is a lovely and popular dessert. It may be served sliced with sweet butter, or served plain as an accompaniment with fruits. My daughters and I often make this French-style honey bread for Christmas presents.

Combine the honey, sugar, and baking soda in a bowl. Heat the water to just barely boiling and add to the honey mixture along with the anise seeds and fruit rind. Stir until blended. Sift the flour and salt. Gradually add to honey mixture. Stir until dough is smooth. The dough will be thickish.

1 cup honey
1 cup sugar
3 tsp. baking soda
1 cup boiling water
grated rind of one orange or one lemon
1 T. crushed anise seeds
1/8 tsp. salt
4 cups flour
butter for pan
2 T. warm milk

It is the custom in France to age this dough overnight in a cool dark place. However, if you are in a hurry it can be baked right away. Butter a 9-inch bread pan or 2 small 7-inch pans. Place the dough in the pan and bake at 350° for one hour. Remove to a rack and brush with the warm milk. Cool and remove from pan.

Beach Cities Irish Soda Bread

I live in Hermosa Beach, which is between Manhattan Beach and Redondo Beach, about 20 minutes south of the Los Angeles airport. These small towns are referred to as the Beach Cities, and each has wonderful swimming and surfing beaches. The towns are mostly residential with downtown areas that include bars and restaurants. On Saint Patrick's Day, the cities celebrate. Nearly everyone wears green T-shirts with various slogans and emblems. Bars offer green beer and restaurants serve corned beef and cabbage. Some make fresh soda bread. This is a wonderful bread that is easy to prepare and popular any day of the year.

In a large bowl, mix together the flour, salt, baking powder, baking soda, sugar, and raisins, if used. Add the butter and cut with a pastry blender until crumbly. Slightly beat the egg, mix with the buttermilk, and add to the dry ingredients. Stir until blended. Turn out on a floured board. Knead until smooth, about 3 minutes. Divide dough in half.

4 cups unsifted white flour (or substitute some wheat flour, if desired)

1 tsp. salt

3 T. baking powder

1 tsp. baking soda

1/4 cup sugar

2 cups raisins or currants (optional)

1/4 cup (1/8 lb) butter

1 egg

1-3/4 cups buttermilk

Shape each into a round loaf. Place each loaf in an 8-inch cake or pie pan. Press down and with a sharp knife cut crosses on top of the loaves (about 1/4 inch deep). Bake at 375° for 35–40 minutes. This will make two medium sized loaves.

Save a piece of the crust for your pocket, as the Irish love folklore and believe in this centuries-old poem:

In your pocket carry a trust,
carry nothing but a crust.
For that holy piece of bread
charms the danger and the dread.

Twenties Soft Gingerbread

Some of my favorite cookbooks are those written in the 1920s by various California ladies' groups to help charitable causes. The style of many of these recipes reflects that, in those days, Mother was at home and in the kitchen, baking. Gingerbread appears in many of these old-fashioned and charming cookbooks. If you have forgotten how wonderful gingerbread can smell and taste, try this traditional recipe, and "may your happiness spread like butter on hot gingerbread."

Sift the flour, baking powder, baking soda, sugar, salt, and spices together. Beat the egg, and add the milk and molasses to it; stir the liquid into the flour mixture. Add the melted butter and combine well. Pour into a well greased loaf pan. Bake at 350° for 30 minutes. This may also be baked in cupcake or muffin tins for 20–25 minutes.

2 cups all-purpose flour
2 tsp. baking powder
1/2 tsp. soda
1/4 cup sugar
1/2 tsp. salt
2 tsp. ground ginger
1 tsp. cinnamon
1 egg
1/2 cup milk
1/2 cup molasses (any kind)
1/4 cup melted butter

Bake Sale Banana Bread

In California there always seems to be some kind of bake sale going on, raising funds for a school, garden club, election campaign, or some neighborhood improvement. This citrus-flavored banana bread has always been a hit at these sales. It is nice for a light dessert or afternoon snack.

Cream the shortening, citrus rind, and sugar together. Add the eggs, one at a time, beating well after each egg.

Sift the dry ingredients and add alternately with the bananas and rum (if used) to make a smooth mixture.

1/3 cup butter or shortening
1 tsp. grated orange or lemon rind
2/3 cup white sugar
2 eggs
1-3/4 cups white flour
1/4 tsp. baking soda
1/2 tsp. salt
2 tsp. baking powder
1 cup mashed bananas (about 2 medium sized)
1 T. rum (optional)

Place the bread batter in a greased 9″ × 5″ × 3″ loaf pan. Bake at 350° for one hour, until golden brown. Place on a rack to cool before removing from pan.

California Avocado Sandwich

Avocados grow easily in California, and are popular in many ways. They are delicious, especially on sandwiches, and contain many vitamins and minerals. Some California ladies rub the avocado seeds on their faces. These seeds contain a natural oil that reputedly rejuvenates the skin.

Mash the avocado. Season to taste with salt, pepper, and minced green onion. Moisten to desired consistency with mayonnaise or sour cream.

ripe avocado
large slices of sourdough bread
Jack or cheddar cheese
salt and pepper to taste
green onion, minced
mayonnaise or sour cream

For each person, lightly butter the bread slices. Top with grated cheddar or Jack cheese. Broil or toast just until the cheese is melted. Top with the avocado. This recipe is a little casual, and the exact portions are left up to the appetite of the cook.

About Sourdough Bread

Bread made with a sourdough starter is part of California cooking history. During the gold rush, miners who were guardians of a starter held a special place in the mining community. In many ways, a starter was as precious as gold. There were no bakeries or food provision stores in those rugged hills. All food had to be carried in on miners' backs or burros. There is a rather incredible story telling of a miner who had his can of starter tied over the back of his burro. The burro slipped and the starter dribbled over the animal's back. The miner scraped whatever he could salvage from the burro's hairy back and returned it to the starter container, hairs, dust, and all. A miner without a starter would be doomed to near starvation.

Housewives up and down the state in the early days of settlement also used sourdough starters. It was kept warm on the back of the wood stove.

What is a starter? It is a mixture of flour and water or milk that is left open to capture wild yeast cells in the air. Various amounts of this added to dough causes the dough to rise and gives that indescribable marvelous "sour" tinge to the bread. San Francisco is known for its sourdough bread because the starter survives perfectly in the cool, even temperatures of the city. Scientists who came to San Francisco to study why this bread tasted better in San Francisco were able to identify a special microorganism in the starter. It was named "Lactobacillus San Francisco."

There are many recipes in cookbooks for making sourdough bread at home. It has been my experience, however, that this is not an easy bread for the home cook. The starter is not always reliable, and ovens and climates vary. My advice is simply to enjoy this bread when you are in San Francisco. Do not leave any in the basket at the restaurant; either eat it up or take it home with you. It freezes quite well.

Summer Picnic Sandwiches

Californias inland valleys can have a fierce, intense heat in the summer. For these hot days, sandwiches with a bottle of chilled beer are often the dinner menu. These sandwiches can be prepared in the morning and tucked away in the refrigerator for the flavors to mingle. The tasty Provençal flavor combination is perfect for a hot summer's day.

Slice the rolls in half. Make a shallow hollow in each half of the roll to give space for the filling. Brush both sides of the rolls with the olive oil and minced garlic.

Layer the bottom half with the ingredients in any order you like. Drizzle the vinegar over the filling and sprinkle with pepper. Close sandwich. Wrap in foil or plastic wrap. Press

4 medium sized French rolls (about 7 inches long)

1/2 cup olive oil

2 cloves garlic, minced

1 green or red pepper, cut in thin strips

1 small red onion, sliced

2 hard-boiled eggs, sliced

1 large can of tuna (12-1/2 oz.)

1/2 cup chopped or sliced black olives

2 oz. anchovies, drained (optional)

3 T. wine vinegar

freshly ground pepper

together and place in the refrigerator with a weight on the top. This can be a heavy frying pan or any handy heavy item. Keep the sandwich weighted for an hour. Remove weight and keep refrigerated until serving time. You can also use a round or long loaf of bread, which can be cut into wedges or sliced.

Sunshine Marmalade Muffins

Marmalade swirled into a muffin batter gives a pleasant orange flavor and a pretty sunshine-flecked appearance. Muffins are very easy to prepare. The procedure is simple—dry ingredients are sifted into a bowl and combined with liquid ingredients. If you want to make muffins for breakfast, the dry ingredients can even be measured out the night before to speed the procedure.

Sift dry ingredients together in a bowl. In another bowl beat the egg and add remaining ingredients. Add dry ingredients to the egg mixture bowl. Mix lightly. Muffin dough should not be overmixed.

2 cups all-purpose flour

1 tsp. baking powder

1/4 tsp. baking soda

1/4 tsp. salt

1/2 tsp. ginger

1/4 cup sugar

1 egg

1/4 cup vegetable oil or melted butter

1 cup buttermilk

1/2 cup marmalade

The batter should be very slightly lumpy. Grease muffin tins well, and fill each cup 2/3 full of the batter. If you use muffin papers, grease the bottom of each cup. Bake at 375° for 25 to 30 minutes. Place on a rack and let rest a minute or two before removing from pan. This will make 12 muffins.

Orange-Scented Scones

Scones have a unique texture and flavor, and have grown quite popular in California bakeries, and also with home bakers. This version has a refreshing citrus taste. Of course, these are perfect with that afternoon cup of tea.

Take 2 T. of flour and mix with the currants or raisins—this prevents them from sinking to the bottom of the scone. Sift the remaining flour with the other dry ingredients. Cut in the butter with a pastry blender until the mixture looks like coarse meal.

Beat the egg with 1 T. water. Add to the flour mixture with the sour cream, currants or raisins, orange juice, and citrus rind.

Divide dough into 24 balls. Flatten, to make round cakes 1/2″ thick. Bake on a greased

1/2 cup currants or raisins
2-1/2 cups sifted flour
1/2 tsp. salt
1/2 cup sugar
2 tsp. baking powder
1 tsp. baking soda
1/3 cup butter (room temperature)
1 egg, beaten with 1 T. water
3/4 cup sour cream
3 T. orange juice
grated rind of 1/2 lemon, 1/2 orange,
    or both

baking sheet for about 12 minutes in a preheated 400° oven, until the scones are golden brown.

If you desire, brush the tops with melted butter before baking. You may also roll this dough out and cut the scones like biscuits. This recipe will make two dozen.

California Pizza

California is a land of fantastic pizzas. They are everywhere, in the finest restaurants, fast-food chains, supermarket aisles, and California kitchens. Pizza is a food nearly everyone adores with a passion. The famous chef Wolfgang Puck tops his pizzas with lamb and duck sausage, smoked salmon with caviar, chanterelles, eggplant and leeks, or spicy chicken strips. With every season there is some new pizza topping trend. Pizza is fun and easy to make in your own kitchen. It is a good beginning cooking procedure for young cooks.

Dissolve the yeast in warm water. Remember, the water should be just warm, not hot. Stir until the yeast is dissolved. Add sugar, salt, and olive oil. Stir in 2 cups of sifted flour. When that is blended in, add the remaining 1-1/2 cups. Knead for a few minutes to blend all the ingredients. Form the dough into a ball and place in a lightly

Basic Pizza Dough
1 pkg. dry yeast
1 cup warm water
1 tsp. sugar
1 tsp. salt
2 T. olive oil
3-1/2 cups flour, sifted

greased bowl. Cover with a dampened towel and set in a warm place, to rise.

When the dough has doubled in size (this will take about 45 minutes) punch it back down. Remove from bowl and roll out in desired pizza shapes. This will make 5 or 6 nine-inch pizzas.

Preheat the oven to 425°. Prepare the pizza top by lightly brushing olive oil over the surface. Top with a thin spreading of tomato sauce; fresh tomatoes peeled and sliced; or crushed canned tomatoes. Next comes your choice of the following, or any other, desired toppings:

Italian sausage, cooked and crumbled. Sardine pieces. Grated mozzarella cheese. Cubes or thin slices of precooked eggplant. Sliced olives, capers, sliced mushrooms, prosciutto, sliced red or white onions, minced garlic, tiny shrimp, minced clams, anchovies, artichoke hearts, etc. A little salt, pepper, oregano, or basil may be sprinkled on top. Bake for 10–15 minutes. I use a pair of kitchen scissors to cut my pizza into desired portions.

Zestful Accompaniments

Imaginative accompaniments can add magic to simple food. I love M.F.K. Fisher's pickled grapes served with cold roast chicken. Lorry's salsa will add extra flavor to barbecued steaks, while peach salsa is lovely with grilled fish. Salsas outsell ketchup in California, offering endless combinations for one to devise.

On some foggy damp evening, try nibbling Ojai cinnamon walnuts with crisp apples and hot tea. Any of the recipes in this chapter can make gifts for friends and family.

M. F. K. Fisher's Pickled Seedless Grapes

My late friend M.F.K. Fisher gave me this unusual grape relish recipe some years ago. It is typical of her uncomplicated, joyful style of cooking.

1-1/2 cups sugar

1 cup white vinegar or white wine vinegar

4 3-inch sticks cinnamon

4 cups seedless grapes (green or flame red), washed and stemmed

4 very clean half-pint canning jars

Place sugar and vinegar in a small saucepan. Bring to a boil and stir. Simmer for 5 minutes. Place grapes in the jars with a cinnamon stick. Pour syrup in each jar. Cap and store in refrigerator for up to 3 weeks. Serve with cold fish, fowl, or cold meats.

Fresh Peach Salsa

Ripe velvety peaches combine with cilantro, red onion, and spices to make this lovely refreshing salsa.

2 ripe peaches, peeled and diced

1/4 cup lime juice

1/2 red onion, finely diced (about 1/4 cup)

1 tsp. ground cumin

1/4 cup minced fresh cilantro

pinch of salt

1/8 tsp. cayenne

1 T. finely minced fresh ginger

Combine ingredients in a pretty bowl. Let mellow for one hour at room temperature. This will serve 6 as a salsa accompaniment to poultry, fish, or meat.

Lorry's Salsa de Jitomate Norte

My friend Lorry shared this family sauce with me many years ago. It comes from northern Mexico and is used on top of steak, oysters, fresh clams, or chicken. The tomatoes are broiled, which gives a character entirely different from salsas made with fresh diced tomatoes.

1 lb fresh tomatoes (medium size)

1 T. finely chopped fresh cilantro

1/4 cup finely chopped onion

3/4 tsp. salt

2 canned peeled green chiles, cut in thin strips (2 fresh peeled Anaheim chiles may also be used)

1-1/2 tsp. white vinegar or white wine vinegar

Line a shallow metal pan with foil. Place the tomatoes in a single layer in it and place under a broiler for about 20 minutes, or until the tops are charred. Do not place too close to the heat source or the tomatoes will burn. Each broiler is different. The idea is to get the tomatoes hot and slightly charred on top. Cool slightly, and place in a blender— seeds, core, skins, everything. This is what gives the sauce its character. Blend the tomatoes until smooth.

Cool the blended tomatoes slightly and place in a serving dish. Add the remaining ingredients, mix together, and wait 30 minutes before serving so the flavors can blend. Serve fresh. This will make around 3 cups of salsa.

Cucumber-Mint Salsa

This combination makes a cooling, invigorating salsa that is especially appealing with poultry or grilled fish.

1 medium cucumber

salt and pepper to taste

1 cup plain yogurt

1/2 cup fresh mint leaves, finely minced

Peel the cucumber, leaving a few slivers of green skin for color. Dice into small cubes. Place in a bowl, season with salt and pepper, and add remaining ingredients. Chill for one hour before serving. This will make around 2 cups.

Pacific Salsa

A colorful combination of tropical fruits makes this a lovely salsa to use with poultry or meats. It may also be used as a topping for sliced fresh fruit.

1 cup peeled and diced kiwi fruit

1 cup diced fresh pineapple (canned may also be used)

1 cup chopped yellow or red bell pepper

1/4 cup fresh lime juice

2 T. white sugar

1/4 cup finely minced fresh cilantro (optional)

Combine all ingredients in a pretty bowl. Mix together and let stand for one hour to mellow, before serving.

Pomegranate Orange Salsa

This is a striking-looking salsa to use as a topping for any meat, fish, or poultry. Pomegranates are not available all year round, so this is a special pomegranate season salsa.

Remove seeds from pomegranate. This is easily done by breaking the pomegranate and placing the pieces in a bowl of water. Release the seeds with your hands. Drain, and pat the seeds dry. Peel the orange and cut it into small pieces. Put the orange and the pomegranate seeds in a bowl. Add the

seeds from 1 large pomegranate, or 2 small (about 3/4 lb)

1 large orange

1 T. finely minced green onion or chive tops

4 T. lime or lemon juice

3 T. finely minced Anaheim chili or canned chilies

2 T. fresh minced parsley

pinch of salt

remaining ingredients and let stand for one hour before serving. This will make about 1-1/2 cups.

Ojai Cinnamon Walnuts

1 cube of salted butter (4 oz.)
4 cups of shelled walnut halves
1/4 cup water
1 cup white sugar
2 T. cinnamon

Ojai is a town tucked back in the hills about an hour from Los Angeles. It is the home of the famed Ojai music festival which takes place every June. The area is renowned for the quality of the walnuts that are grown there.

A local walnut grower developed this recipe for holiday presents. These walnuts are delicious to nibble on a cool night, with hot coffee or tea.

Melt the butter over a low flame in a small frying pan. Remove from heat and add walnuts, stirring to coat evenly. In another frying pan (iron works very well) combine the water, sugar, and cinnamon. Heat the ingredients just until they come to a simmer. Add the pan of walnuts and butter to the sugar-cinnamon mixture. Stir ingredients with a wooden spoon constantly until the sugar-cinnamon mixture has adhered to the walnuts. Spread out in a single layer on a piece of aluminum foil. Cool and store in glass jars for presents or snacking. This will make 4 cups.

Desserts

Pies, Cakes, Cookies, and Other Sweet Things

Desserts are the sweet finale to any meal. In California, they are innovative and diverse, often flavored with the state's oranges and lemons, walnuts and dates. The style of California desserts has always tended more towards lightness and smaller portions than in other areas of America.

There are no hard-and-fast rules about the proper dessert to serve. I have been at birthday parties where a cheese pie is served instead of a birthday cake. Cupcakes are often served at a children's birthday party as they are easier for young hands to handle. Cookies are very popular and are often served with a bowl of fresh seasonal fruit. School children and working adults like to tuck a few cookies in with their lunches for a treat. A slice of walnut torte may be offered at a brunch. The choice is yours!

219

Schooltime Cupcakes

My three children all went to the nearby grammar school. It is important, and fun, for parents to be involved in school activities, and in my case this included making cupcakes for various events. I have tried many recipes, and this one is so quick and easy your children could make them.

1-1/2 cups all-purpose flour

2/3 cup sugar

2 tsp. baking powder

1/2 tsp. salt

1/3 cup vegetable shortening

1/2 cup milk

1-1/2 tsp. vanilla

1 egg

Sift flour, sugar, baking powder, and salt into a mixing bowl. Add the shortening, milk, and vanilla, and beat one and a half minutes by hand or with a mixer. Add the egg and beat another one and a half minutes. With a scraper, scrape the sides of the bowl and make sure the dough is well blended.

Bake in paper cupcake cups or lightly greased metal cupcake pans at 375° for 15–20 minutes. Frost as desired, or use the following recipe:

Bittersweet Cupcake Frosting

---

5 oz. semisweet chocolate

2 T. butter

1-1/2 cups sifted confectioner's sugar

1/8 tsp. salt

1/4 cup milk

1 tsp. vanilla

Melt chocolate and butter together in a double boiler over hot water. Remove from heat and add the remaining ingredients, stirring until thick enough to spread. Top the frosting with half a walnut, if desired. This will make enough frosting for 12 large or 18 small cupcakes.

Lemon Daffodil Cake

It is a popular misconception that California does not have distinct seasons. This is not true! Anyone who has been in a Sierra snowstorm, or driven up the coast on Highway One with spring's golden poppies and lavender-hued lupine clinging to rocky cliffs will know each month brings new changes.

In springtime in Santa Barbara, the stream in Rocky Nook Park is full and bubbling. Children scamper over the slippery rocks and dip tiny toes in the cool water. Century-old sycamores show new green foliage, and the picnic tables are full. This light spring cake fits in perfectly for an April birthday.

This cake is made with two batters, one white and one yellow. They are spooned into the pan to create little pockets of yellow (daffodils) among the white.

There are two very important keys to success with this cake. The first is having the egg whites at room temperature. To do this, separate the whites from the yolks and leave them out of the refrigerator for one hour.

The White Batter

1-3/4 cups egg whites (12–14 eggs)
1-1/4 cups sifted cake flour
1-1/2 cups sugar
1/2 tsp. salt
1-1/2 tsp. cream of tartar
1-1/2 tsp. vanilla extract

The Daffodil Batter

5 egg yolks
2 T. cake flour
2 T. sugar
2 T. grated lemon peel

Frosting

Lemon glaze (powdered sugar mixed with lemon juice) or sifted confectioner's sugar

The other key is that you MUST use cake flour, and resift it three times.

To begin the white batter, sift the flour with 1/2 cup of the sugar THREE TIMES.

221

With an electric mixer or hand whisk, beat the egg whites, with salt and cream of tartar, to soft peak stage. Next, beat in 1 cup of sugar, 1/4 cup at a time. Beat well after each addition. It should form stiff peaks. With a wire whisk, fold in the vanilla.

Now sift the flour mixture, one fourth at a time, into the egg whites. Using an over and under motion, very gently fold in each addition of flour. This will take 10 strokes each time.

Leave the egg white mixture in the bowl while you prepare the daffodil mixture. Combine the egg yolks, cake flour, sugar, and lemon peel. Beat with an electric mixer or hand whisk until very thick. Add to this mixture one third of the white mixture and blend with a whisk.

Preheat oven to 375°.

Take a 10-inch tube pan (angel cake pans do not require greasing). Spoon in white and yellow batter alternately. With a knife, cut through batter twice. Take a rubber scraper and gently spread the batter in the pan until the top is smooth and the sides are even.

Bake for 35 to 40 minutes. The top should spring back when pressed with a fingertip. Remove it from the oven and hang the pan upside down over the neck of a bottle for 2 hours. This keeps the cake from collapsing. Loosen the cake from pan with a spatula and place it on a cake plate. Glaze, or dust with confectioner's sugar. This cake will serve 10.

California Sunshine Orange Cake

Many people still think of California as all orange groves and perpetual sunshine. It is true the sun does shine a lot here, and there are plenty of orange groves, mostly in the southern part of the state. I have orange trees in my back yard, as do many Californians. In the spring, the scent of the blossoms is exhilarating. During the December holidays I pick oranges from the trees. Many California recipes take advantage of this abundance of oranges. This light, delicate, orange-flavored cake is especially nice served with seasonal fresh fruit.

Beat the egg whites with cream of tartar, adding 1/2 a cup of sugar 2 tablespoons at a time, until the whites are stiff. Remember, egg whites should be at room temperature before beating. Set the whites aside.

Next, beat the egg yolks until they are thick and lemon colored. Gradually add the remaining 1 cup of sugar, mixing until well

6 egg whites, at room temperature

1/2 tsp. cream of tartar

1-1/2 cups sugar

6 egg yolks

1 T. grated orange rind

1-1/2 cups flour (cake flour is recommended)

1 tsp. salt

1/2 cup orange juice (about 2 medium oranges)

blended and somewhat thick. Stir in the orange rind.

Sift flour and salt together. Add, alternately with the orange juice, to egg yolks. Fold orange mixture gently into egg whites. Pour into a 10-inch ungreased tube pan. Bake in a 325° oven for one hour or until cake springs back when touched with your fingertips. Invert pan immediately on a wire rack. Allow the cake to cool completely. Loosen it with a spatula and shake the cake out of the pan. An orange glaze made with orange juice and powdered sugar may be spread on top, if desired.

Mocha Chocolate Cake

Chocolate and coffee mingled together are a most tantalizing flavor combination. This is a good easy recipe for beginning cooks; with this very simple cake making method, it is possible to bake a cake from scratch in just about the same time as it takes with a boxed mix. I have used this delicious cake for many birthday parties.

Sift dry ingredients together in a mixing bowl.

Add shortening, 1/3 cup buttermilk, and coffee. Beat for two minutes, then add remaining buttermilk, eggs, and vanilla. This will be a smooth batter. Pour into two greased and floured 8- or 9-inch cake pans. Bake at 350° for 30 to 35 minutes. Frost with your choice of frosting, or simply sift powdered sugar over the top.

2 cups white flour
1 tsp. baking soda
1 tsp. salt
1 tsp. cinnamon
1/2 cup cocoa
1-1/2 cups sugar

Add:

1/2 cup shortening
1/3 cup buttermilk or sour milk
1/2 cup cooled strong coffee

Then add:

1/3 cup buttermilk or sour milk
2 eggs
1 tsp. vanilla or rum

Julian Applesauce Cake

The historic town of Julian is tucked back in the Cuyamaca mountains behind the coastal city of Oceanside. Placer gold was discovered there in 1870, and for several years there was a gold mining fever. Many of the miners became disenchanted and realized that the real gold could be found in farming at this 4200-foot elevation. The climate is ideal for apple and pear trees, and in the fall, the ranches offer freshly picked apples and apple cider. There is an apple festival, with restaurants and stands offering special food and crafts. Applesauce gives extra flavor and moistness to this tasty, healthy cake.

Cream shortening or butter with sugar, spices, and cocoa until light and fluffy. Add the eggs one at a time, mixing well after each addition.

1/2 cup butter or shortening

1 cup brown sugar

1/2 tsp. cinnamon

1/2 tsp. cloves

1/2 tsp. nutmeg

1/4 tsp. salt

2 T. powdered cocoa

2 eggs, unbeaten

2 cups sifted flour

1-1/2 tsp. baking soda

1-1/2 cups applesauce

3/4 cup raisins and 3/4 cup chopped walnuts (optional)

Sift the flour and baking soda together. Add the dry ingredients to the creamed mixture alternately with the applesauce (and raisins and nuts, if used). Bake in a greased 10″ × 10″ × 2″ baking pan at 350° for 1 hour. Remove the cake from the pan and serve it either plain or with any simple frosting.

Karen's Ojai Walnut Torte

Karen was a college roommate of my daughter, Jeanne. She was from Ojai, a small town nestled in a valley behind the Santa Barbara coast. Ojai is famous for its music festival and quiet country life amidst orchards, including walnut trees. Karen would bring this torte to recital parties, where it was very popular. Torte is just a German word for a cake made with many eggs.

Melt the butter and let it cool slightly. Beat the egg whites with salt until soft peaks form. Gradually add the powdered sugar, beating until stiff but not dry.

In a separate bowl, beat the egg yolks slightly. Add the sugar and vanilla, and beat until thick and creamy. Sprinkle the flour over the egg whites. Add the egg yolks and gently fold until the mixture is half blended. Add the butter and 3/4 cup of the walnuts. Fold just until mixed. This is delicate, and it is important not to overmix.

1/3 cup butter
6 egg whites
1/2 tsp. salt
3 T. powdered sugar
6 egg yolks
1 cup granulated sugar
3 tsp. vanilla
1-1/2 cups sifted all-purpose flour
1 cup chopped walnuts

Pour into a well buttered and floured 2-1/2 or 3 quart cake mold, or a 10-inch tube pan. Top with the remaining walnuts and bake at 350° for 40 minutes. The torte should bounce back when you touch it.

Cool the torte for 10 minutes in the pan. Then pierce the cake in several places with a long skewer and pour the rum sauce (recipe follows) over the torte. This will take 10 minutes of on-and-off pouring to absorb the sauce. Place on a serving plate. This will serve 10.

Rum Sauce

1-1/2 cups granulated sugar
1-1/2 cups warm water
dash of salt
grated rinds of 1/2 orange and 1/2 lemon
1/3 cup rum

Combine all ingredients in a saucepan, except the rum. Bring the mixture to a boil and simmer over a low flame for 10 minutes. Cool, and stir in the rum.

Walnut-Raisin-Orange Cozy Cake

This is the kind of flavorful healthy cake you might make for your mother or an aunt. As a child, I used to help my mother make cakes. We used a sturdy Sunbeam mixer and she always warned me to be careful not to get my hands near the beaters. I have always heeded her advice, and am happy to say I've never had an accident with the beaters.

1 cup brown sugar
1/2 cup butter (room temperature)
2 eggs
1 tsp. vanilla or rum
2 cups flour
1 tsp. baking soda
1/2 tsp. salt
1 cup buttermilk
1 cup raisins
1/2 cup chopped walnuts
peel from 1 orange

(continued on next page)

(continued from previous page)

Cream the butter and sugar together until light and fluffy. Add the eggs and vanilla and mix well. Sift the flour, baking soda, and salt together. Add the sifted ingredients to the creamed mixture alternately with the buttermilk. Mix until blended. Finely chop the raisins, orange peel, and walnuts, and stir into the mixture.

Lightly grease and flour a 9″ × 9″ × 2″ or 13″ × 9″ × 2″ baking pan. Pour in the cake batter. Bake in a 350° oven for 45 to 50 minutes. The top should bounce back when pressed with your finger.

Orange Glaze

1/2 cup orange juice
1/2 cup white sugar

While the cake is baking, heat the orange juice and sugar together. Stir and simmer until the sugar is dissolved. A dash of rum may be added, if desired.

When the cake is done, remove it from the oven and place the pan on a cake rack. Prick the top of the cake with a fork. Dribble the glaze over it. Cut in squares to serve from the pan, or remove from pan and serve on a pretty plate.

Jenny's White Wine Wedding Cake

Weddings in California are often held out-doors. Our friend Jenny's wedding was in a valley garden, where the vows were exchanged under spreading trees. Guests sipped champagne, danced, and dined on a beautiful buffet lunch.

My daughter Jeanne and other close friends prepared the wedding cake. This has become a tradition, an offering of special caring among friends. It has not always been easy; cakes have slipped in the car on the way to the wedding, cracks mysteriously appear in cakes, and frostings become runny. But these are cakes from the heart, and they are repaired with flowers filling cracks, skewers holding up the layers, and extra frosting wherever it may be needed. This is a favorite among many such cakes. The white wine adds a tantalizing flavor and moistness.

2 cups sugar

4 eggs

2-1/2 cups cake flour (all-purpose may substituted)

1/2 tsp. baking powder

1 cup vegetable oil

1 cup dry white wine

1 tsp. vanilla

In a mixing bowl, beat the eggs and sugar together for 30 seconds. Sift the dry ingredients together. Add the oil, wine, vanilla, and dry ingredients to the egg mixture. Mix for one minute, making sure everything is blended. Grease and flour two 9″ cake pans, pour in batter and bake at 350° for 30 minutes. Remove from cake pans and cool on racks. Frost as desired. For wedding cakes, repeat this recipe as many times as needed.

Dessert Honey Cake

I know several beekeepers in California. They are all calm, gentle people, and are generous with their honey, giving it as a special gift to their friends. It is an interesting bit of honey trivia that bees must travel more than twice the distance around the world to collect enough nectar for a pound of honey. Honey was the first sweetener ever used by man.

One of my beekeeper friends shared this special, delicately flavored recipe with me.

Cream the butter and sugar together until fluffy. Stir in the beaten eggs, then mix in the honey and blend. Sift the dry ingredients together, and add gradually, along with the orange rind and applesauce. Lastly stir in the walnuts, if used.

3 T. butter (room temperature)
1/2 cup sugar
3 eggs, well beaten
3/4 cup honey
2 cups sifted flour
1 tsp. baking powder
1 tsp. baking soda
1/4 tsp. salt
grated rind of 1 orange
1/2 cup applesauce
1 cup chopped walnuts (optional)

Bake in a well greased oblong pan (about 12″ × 9″ × 2″) at 325° for 40 to 45 minutes. The sides should slightly come away from the pan. This is not a big, high cake.

Cool on a rack and cut into squares to serve. If desired, sweet butter may be served to spread on the cake.

Mama's North Beach Cheese Pie

Every Italian mother has her secret recipes for tempting sweets. Peek in any of San Francisco's North Beach bakery windows and you will see cheese pies in the refrigerated glass dessert cases, just waiting for you to order a slice. Paired with a cup of fresh espresso, this can be a relaxing way to enjoy a little interlude in North Beach. This recipe, with a whisper of lemon flavor, is a traditional favorite.

Melt the butter, mix with the crumbs, sugar, and cinnamon, and press into a 9-inch pie pan. Bake at 375° for 8 minutes.

Cream the cheese with the sugar until smooth. Add the eggs and again beat until smooth. Blend in the salt and lemon. Fill the baked crust with this mixture. Bake at 325° for 30 minutes. Remove from the oven.

Mix the topping ingredients together. Carefully spread on top of the pie. Bake an additional 30 minutes at 350°. Cool and refrigerate. This pie may be served as is, or garnished with colorful jam, fresh berries, or thin lemon slices. This will serve 8–10.

Crust

1/3 cup butter

1-1/2 cups graham cracker crumbs (about 11 single crackers)

1/4 cup sugar

1/4 tsp. cinnamon

Filling

2 8-oz. pkgs. (1 lb) cream cheese, at room temperature

1/2 cup sugar

2 eggs

1/8 tsp. salt

1 tsp. finely grated lemon rind or 1 tsp. lemon juice

Topping

1 cup sour cream

2 T. sugar

1 tsp. vanilla

Golden State Lemon Meringue Pie

Lemon groves have been a part of California's heritage since the Spanish planted the first trees in the state. Lemons have always been an important ingredient in California cuisine.

This classic pie recipe gets an extra tang from the addition of the lemon rind. The pie is at its absolute best when baked a few hours before dessert time, and served at cool room temperature to enhance the flavor.

In a heavy saucepan, mix the sugar, cornstarch, and water. Blend together over medium heat, stirring until thickish. Gently mix in the egg yolks and blend well. Lower the heat and add the butter, lemon juice, and rind. Cook for a minute. Remove from heat. Stir and cool slightly. Pour into the pie shell. Top with meringue.

pie shell of your choice (to fit a 9-inch pie)
1-1/2 cups sugar
1/3 cup cornstarch
1-1/2 cups water
3 egg yolks, slightly beaten
3 T. butter
4 T. lemon juice (1 medium lemon)
grated rind from one lemon

Meringue

3 egg whites
1/4 tsp. cream of tartar
6 T. sugar

Beat egg whites with cream of tartar until frothy. Gradually beat in the sugar, and continue beating until the whites are stiff. Spoon over the pie. Bake at 400° for 10 minutes. The top should be golden brown. Cool on a rack, away from drafts.

San Francisco Chocolate Rum Pie

Rum has been used in San Francisco recipes since the early drinking days of the city. Miners enjoyed using their gold to buy intoxicating beverages—in 1860 there were 800 groggeries in the city. Drinking tastes have moved from hard liquor to fine wines over the years, but chocolate pie flavored with rum remains a popular and seductive favorite.

Melt the chocolate chips in a double boiler or heavy pan over a low flame. Cool slightly. Add the one whole egg, plus two egg yolks and rum, and mix well with a mixer at low speed. Beat the remaining egg whites in a separate bowl with a mixer until stiff. Fold into the chocolate mixture.

1 9-inch baked and cooked pie shell (a graham cracker crust is a good choice for this pie)
1 6-oz. pkg. chocolate chips
3 eggs (2 separated)
3 T. dark or light rum
1 pint whipping cream

Whip the cream until fairly stiff. Blend one cup of the cream into the pie mixture. Reserve the remaining cup for the pie top. Carefully spoon the filling into the pie shell and refrigerate. To serve, spread the remaining cup of whipped cream over the pie. If desired, garnish with a few chocolate shavings. This will serve 6.

Lake Country Poached Pears

On quiet roads in the northern California lake country, some of the loveliest scenery you will see is miles of pear orchards growing beside vineyards. Poached pears are a refreshing California dessert favorite. I have included two methods of poaching them here. Both are excellent, and will fill your kitchen with heavenly aromas.

Lemon Flavored Poached Pears

4 ripe pears (Bartlett or D'Anjou work
   well)
1 lemon, juice and grated rind
3 cups water
2 cups granulated sugar
1 tsp. vanilla

Combine the lemon juice, rind, water, sugar, and vanilla in a saucepan. Peel the pears, leaving the stems on, and place in the liquid. Give a little stir. Bring to a simmer. Cover and poach gently until the pears are slightly tender, about 8–10 minutes. Do not overcook. If the liquid does not completely cover the pears, roll them around during the cooking. Remove cover and cool. Refrigerate in liquid until serving time.

Raspberry Cardinal Sauce

1-1/2 to 2 cups fresh or frozen
   raspberries
2 T. sugar
1 T. rum, kirsch, or Grand Marnier

If berries are frozen, thaw them. If fresh, wash gently. The size of fresh baskets and frozen packages varies, but don't worry, a few berries more or less will not matter. With a wooden spoon, or whatever works for you, press the berries through a strainer.

This eliminates the seeds. Processors and blenders do not work for this seed-free sauce. Add the sugar and liquor to the sauce and stir. Refrigerate until needed. To serve, drain the poached pears and stand them upright in a dish. Dribble the sauce over them. This will serve 4.

Belle-Helene Chocolate Sauce

2 1-oz. squares of bittersweet chocolate
1/4 cup cream
1 T. butter
1 tsp. vanilla, cognac, or rum

In a double boiler or pot, melt the chocolate with the cream over low heat. Stir in the butter and blend. Add the flavoring. Pour the sauce while slightly warm over the pears. The pear may be placed on a flattened scoop of vanilla ice cream if desired. This will make 4 servings.

Red Wine Poached Pears

This is used by wineries for special parties. The red wine gives the pears a deep rosy glow and adds a nice zing.

4 ripe pears
1 lemon, juice and grated rind
3 cups dry red wine
1 cup sugar
1 tsp. cinnamon

Peel the pears, leaving stems on. Combine the remaining ingredients in a saucepan, stir, and add pears. Give another stir and simmer, covered, just until barely tender (about 8–10 minutes). Stir once while cooking so the liquid will color and flavor all parts of the pears. Cool the pears in the syrup, and serve either chilled or at room temperature.

Daddy's Cream Puffs

When I was growing up with a younger sister and a mother who stayed at home, we liked to do nice things for my daddy. He loved us all very much and we were a happy family. Cream puffs made things even happier. For some reason, people think cream puffs are difficult. They are actually easy to make, but most impressive for any occasion.

In a heavy saucepan, bring the water, butter, and salt to a boil. Remove from the heat. Stir in the cup of flour, all at once. Return the pot to the stove and stir with a wooden spoon over a low heat until the mixture forms a ball. It will pull away from the pan. Remove from heat. Stir in the eggs, one at a time. Beat well after each addition. The mixture will be very smooth, like velvet.

1 cup water
1/2 cup butter (1 cube–4 oz.)
1/4 tsp. salt
1 cup sifted white flour
4 eggs
1 pint whipping cream, whipped and
*   sweetened to taste*

This recipe will make 8 puffs. Drop the batter from a spoon onto an ungreased baking sheet, 3 inches apart. Bake at 400° for 45 minutes, until dry and golden brown. Remove the puffs from the baking sheet to a rack and let cool, away from drafts.

When the puffs are cool, split each in half and fill with whipped cream. Smaller size puffs may be made if you prefer.

Simple Orange Dessert

4 large Valencia or navel oranges
1/4 cup sugar
1 tsp. cinnamon

There are situations when one runs out of cooking time and, alas, there is no dessert. I can remember my mother solving this problem by simply slicing fresh oranges and sprinkling them with sugar and a dash of cinnamon. This is not only simple and refreshing but is also healthy and nutritious.

Oranges are native to South China. They spread west to Europe in the fifth century. Columbus took orange seeds to Haiti, and Spanish settlers carried them to Florida around 1585. The first plantings in California were in Mission gardens in 1769. Four hundred orange trees were planted at the San Gabriel Mission, where some still remain in the mission gardens.

Peel the oranges and slice thinly. Place in a pretty bowl. Sprinkle with sugar and cinnamon, mix well, cover and chill until ready to serve. If desired, garnish with a few sprigs of fresh mint. This will serve 4.

Refreshing California Flan

Slippery and cool, flan is traditionally served after a hot and spicy Mexican meal. Flan recipes are often complicated, with burning sugar and strained mixtures. This is an easy method from a garden club friend, who made it for one of our June lunches.

Beat eggs with hand beater or mixer until well blended. Add sugar and salt. Beat in the milk and vanilla.

Sift the brown sugar into the bottom of a bread pan (9″ × 5″ × 3″) or a square 8″ or 9″ pan. Pour the custard gently into the pan.

8 eggs
2/3 cup granulated sugar
1/4 tsp. salt
2 12-oz. cans of evaporated milk
2 tsp. vanilla
1/3 cup light brown sugar

Heat oven to 350°. Place the flan pan into another shallow baking pan containing warm water. Bake, uncovered, for one hour, or until a knife inserted in the center comes out clean. Refrigerate overnight. Before serving, run a knife around the edge of the pan. Place a serving plate upside down over the pan. Turn over carefully, holding the plate and pan together. The flan may be unmolded ahead of time and kept refrigerated. This will serve 8.

Fresno Apricot Bars

For many holidays and vacations through the years, we have loaded up the car with all the various things a family of five needs to camp in Yosemite. We leave early in the morning, stop for a big hearty breakfast in Bakersfield, and then take Highway 99 through the San Joaquin Valley. The valley is filled with fruit orchards. In the summer heat, we stop at a fruit stand and buy beautiful ripe apricots to eat in the car, and also dried apricots, perfect for trail munching. I buy extra fruit to take home so I can make these irresistible apricot bars.

Cover the dried apricots with water in a saucepan and simmer uncovered for 10 minutes. Drain and cool.

Mix the butter with the white sugar and one cup of the flour. Blend with your hands or a fork until the mixture is crumbly.

Lightly butter an 8″ pan. Press the crumbly mixture into the bottom of the pan. Bake at 350° for 25 minutes.

2/3 cup dried apricots
1/2 cup butter (4 oz.) at room
  temperature
1/4 cup white sugar
1 cup brown sugar
2 eggs, well beaten
1-1/3 cups all-purpose flour, sifted
1/2 tsp. baking powder
1/4 tsp. salt
1/2 tsp. vanilla or rum
1/2 cup walnuts, chopped

While this is baking, add the brown sugar to the beaten eggs and beat together until well blended. Sift the remaining 1/3 cup of flour together with the baking powder and salt. Chop the apricots coarsely and add to egg mixture, along with the flavoring, nuts, and flour mixture.

When the bottom "crust" has baked, remove from oven and spread the apricot mixture over it. Return the pan to the oven and bake at the same temperature an additional 25 minutes. Cool the pan on a rack. Cut into squares or bars.

Cooling Lemon Milk Sherbet

This is just the perfect dessert for a hot day. Fresh summer fruits may be served with it. One nice combination is juicy ripe peaches, diced and dribbled over the top of the sherbet. This is a very uncomplicated recipe; you do not need a machine or any special equipment.

1/2 cup fresh lemon juice (strained)
2 cups sugar
4 cups milk

Mix juice, sugar, and milk and blend well. Place in a stainless steel bowl and put in the freezer for at least four hours. To serve, remove from bowl with metal spoon and dish into individual bowls. This will make 4–6 servings.

Hollywood Hermit Cookies

When I was a teenager I developed papillomas on the bottoms of my feet. These are little hard spots that hurt when you walk on them. It was thought that they were caused by stone bruises, and I did like to walk barefoot, especially around the rocky shore of Lake Wrightwood in the San Bernardino Mountains.

The cure at that time was doses of X rays on these painful patches. The foot doctor had his office on Hollywood Boulevard. I would take the Crenshaw bus for my weekly appointments after school. I was always hungry, so my mother would send some cookies along with me. Often they were an old-fashioned cookie called hermits. I liked to nibble these cookies as I walked slowly along the boulevard watching the colorful local people.

I always expected to see Tyrone Power, Shirley Temple, or some other famous star strolling beside me. It never happened. The treatments in the stuffy dark room were boring, and I was always happy to be finished so I could return to the boulevard and my hermit cookies.

Cream the butter and sugar together until light and fluffy. Add the eggs, one at a time, and blend well. Add the sour cream and baking soda.

Sift the flour, cinnamon, nutmeg, and salt together. Stir into batter and mix well. Now add the raisins and nuts and blend together.

Drop from a teaspoon on a greased cookie sheet. Bake at 350° for 12–15 minutes. The

2/3 cup butter

1 cup brown sugar

2 eggs

2 T. sour cream

1/2 tsp. baking soda

1-3/4 cups flour

1 tsp. cinnamon

1/2 tsp. nutmeg

1/2 tsp. salt

1 cup raisins

1 cup chopped walnuts

cookies should be golden brown. This recipe will make about 3 dozen hermits.

Central Valley Currant Cookies

Currants are dried raisins from special small grape varieties. In California they are grown and dried in the immense Central Valley. Currants have an interesting tang that makes this cookie special.

Serving tea has again become popular in hotels and homes recently. This cookie makes a perfect addition to the tea table.

Place the currants in a bowl. Pour the brandy over the currants and mix together. Let the currants soak for 30 minutes. Drain and reserve the brandy.

Cream butter with sugar until light and fluffy. Add the egg and 2 tablespoons of the brandy (the rest of the brandy can be used in soup) and the currants. Mix well. Sift the flour, salt, nutmeg, and cinnamon together, and blend into the dough. Chill for one hour.

1 cup currants
1-1/2 cups brandy
1 cup sweet butter at room temperature
1 cup sugar
1 egg
2-1/2 cups flour
1/4 tsp. salt
1/2 tsp. nutmeg
1 tsp. cinnamon

Take small pieces of the chilled dough and make little balls about 1 inch in diameter. A little flour rubbed on your hands will make this easy. Place the balls on a buttered cookie sheet about 2 inches apart.

Flatten each cookie with a fork, making a criss-cross design. Bake at 350° for 10–12 minutes or until pale brown. Remove to a rack and cool. Store in airtight containers. This will make about 5 dozen little cookies.

Clare Creighton's Jam Bars

California has a very strong network of garden clubs. These clubs work to preserve special beautiful places in California and to promote various conservation projects. The club members, men and women of all ages, have worked together to save parks, plant trees, and create native gardens. Once a year, our Hermosa Beach Garden Club has a plant sale and lunch to raise funds for gardens and conservation needs. One of the club's favorite cookies for this lunch is from Clare Crieghton. While she has passed on, her cookie recipe is used and treasured by all of us.

Cream the sugar and butter together. Add the egg yolk and blend. Stir in the flour and salt. Pat the dough in a thin layer in a pan (about 9" × 12" or close). You may use a fork to pat the dough down.

Cookie Dough

1/2 lb sweet butter

1/2 cup sugar

1 egg yolk

2-1/2 cups flour

1/2 tsp. salt

Topping

4 egg whites

1 cup sugar

1 cup black currant jelly, apricot jam, or other

1 cup chopped walnuts

Beat the egg whites. Gradually add the sugar to make a stiff meringue. Spread the jam or jelly over dough. Spread meringue over jelly. Sprinkle walnuts over top. Bake at 350°until meringue is crisp and golden brown, about 25 to 30 minutes. Cool and cut into squares.

Guenoc Brownies from Karen Melander-Magoon

The Guenoc Winery, with 300 acres of vineyards and a wonderful wine tasting room, is located in one of the most beautiful valleys in California. This was the home of the famous Victorian actress and great beauty, Lillie Langtry. Her home has been carefully preserved, and is open for special events.

Karen Melander-Magoon, Guenoc's marketing and education director, has great style in matching food with wine. Her delicious brownies, served with Guenoc Petite Sirah, form a winning combination.

Preheat oven to 350°. Butter an 8- or 9-inch square cake pan (you may find buttering only the bottom works best). Melt the choco-

3 oz. unsweetened chocolate
6 T. butter
1-1/2 cups sugar
3 eggs
1/4 tsp. salt
3/4 cup flour
1 cup chopped walnuts
1-1/2 tsp. vanilla

late and butter together in a double boiler or in a pan over simmering water, stirring until smooth. Remove from heat. Stir in sugar, eggs, salt, flour, walnuts and vanilla. Combine well.

Spread the mixture in the pan. Bake for 35 to 40 minutes, until dry on top and almost firm to the touch. Set the pan on a rack to cool for about 15 minutes, then cut the brownies in 2-1/4 inch squares. Serve slightly warm, with a Guenoc Petite Sirah.

Guenoc Brownies From Jackie

This is yet another recipe from the Guenoc winery. Jackie, their hospitality chairman, created this unusual version using macadamia nuts. They add a magical crunch to these terrific brownies.

Melt the chocolate and butter in a double boiler. Remove to a bowl, cool slightly, add beaten eggs and mix well. Next add sugar, vanilla, and brandy. Mix well. Add the flour, half a cup at a time. Add the nuts. Pour into a buttered 11″ × 18″ baking dish. This size pan is known as a jelly roll pan. If you do not have one, simply divide the dough between two 8″ square pans. Bake at 350° for 55 minutes. Do not overcook. Cool on a rack and cut in squares. At the tasting room at Guenoc, Petite Sirah is served with Jackie's brownies.

10 oz. sweet chocolate

3 4-oz. cubes sweet butter

6 eggs, beaten

4 cups sugar

1 T. vanilla

1 oz. brandy

2 cups unbleached or all-purpose flour

2 cups chopped macadamia nuts

Peanut Butter Cookies

When I was about 6, my father, who was a sports reporter for *The Los Angeles Times*, fell asleep on the way home to Hermosa Beach, and his car hit a telephone pole. He had been reporting on a late night basketball game. Fortunately, he only received some bruises, but this event made my mother decide it was time to move closer to his work. Our new neighborhood, in South West Los Angeles, was friendly, and soon I had all kinds of new friends. One of these, Charles, had a mother who made peanut cookies. She handed them out to all the local children and we loved them. This is her recipe.

1/2 cup butter or shortening
1/2 cup peanut butter (chunky or smooth)
3/4 cup brown sugar
1 egg
1 tsp. vanilla
1-1/4 cups flour
1/2 tsp. baking powder
3/4 tsp. baking soda
1/4 tsp. salt
peanuts for top (optional)

Cream the butter, peanut butter, sugar, egg, and vanilla together until smooth and well blended. Sift the flour, baking powder, salt, and baking soda together, and mix into the first mixture. Chill the dough for easier handling. Roll into balls about the size of a walnut and place on a lightly greased cookie sheet. Dip a fork in cold water and flatten each cookie, making a criss-cross design. If desired, press a peanut in the center of each cookie.

Bake at 375° for 10–12 minutes. Cool on racks and store in an airtight container. This will make about 40 cookies.

Lemon Snow Bars

Lemons were grown in the mission gardens, and have been always been used in California baking for extra flavor. These lemon snow bars make a refreshing ending for a dinner. The "snow" is powdered sugar drifted on the tops of the bars.

To make the crust, cream the butter and sugar together in a bowl. Sift the flour and salt together, and blend into the butter mixture. Mix until smooth, press lightly into a 13″ × 9″ × 2″ baking pan, and bake in a 350° oven for 20 minutes. Remove from the oven.

Combine the topping ingredients, except for the powdered sugar, and mix until smooth. Pour over the baked crust. Return to the oven and bake an additional 25 minutes. Cool in the pan, on a rack.

When cool, sift on the powdered sugar "snow" and cut into desired size bars. This recipe can be cut in half, and baked in a 9″ square pan, to make a smaller amount. The full recipe will make about 3 dozen bars.

Crust

1 cup butter (at room temperature)

1/2 cup powdered sugar

2 cups sifted flour

1/2 tsp. salt

1/2 cup finely chopped walnuts or hazel nuts (optional)

Topping

4 eggs

1-1/2 cups sugar

1/4 cup flour

1 tsp. baking powder

1/2 cup lemon juice (2 medium sized lemons, or close)

2 tsp. grated lemon rind

1/4 tsp. salt

1/4 cup sifted powdered sugar for the "snow"

They will keep in an airtight container for several days or in the refrigerator for a week.

Date Nut Bars

Once I flew in a tiny Cessna airplane to the desert town of Indio with friends to attend the annual date festival. This town is renowned for date trees. As you approach the city from the air, the rows of trees in the date groves come into view, making a fascinating design of intricately woven green lines. On the ground are many booths selling dates prepared in various ways: chopped, pitted, stuffed, date shakes, and many more. There is a parade with camels, and the local people dress up in date-ethnic garb. Indio dates are very popular in California cooking.

These date bars are quick and easy to make. It is a good recipe for young cooks, as it is mixed by hand in one bowl.

> 1 cup flour
> 1 tsp. baking powder
> 1 tsp. salt
> 2 cups dark brown sugar
> 1 tsp. vanilla
> 2 eggs, beaten
> 1/2 cup chopped walnuts
> 1 cup dates, pitted and cut in small pieces

Sift flour, baking powder, and salt together in a bowl. Add brown sugar, eggs, and vanilla. Beat until smooth. This may be done by hand with a fork or spoon. Add dates and walnuts and blend. Place the dough in a greased 8″ square pan. Bake at 350° for 20–25 minutes, or until the top is brown and firm. Cool in the pan on a rack for 5 minutes. Cut into bars of desired size. These bars may be sprinkled with powdered sugar if desired.

Yummy Chocolate Wafers

Who can resist a chocolate cookie? It is even possible to bake a batch and then sit down and eat them all, right down to the last crumb. These cookies are irresistible. They make a nice gift for someone special. This method of dropping the batter on a baking sheet and then pressing it down with a damp towel over a glass is easy and fun.

Melt the chocolate and cool slightly. Combine the shortening, salt, and vanilla in a mixing bowl. Add the sugar slowly, and mix well. Add the eggs one a time, beating well after each addition. Add the chocolate and again mix well. Blend in the flour and nuts, until the mixture is smooth. Drop from a tablespoon onto lightly greased cookie sheets.

---

3 oz. semisweet chocolate

1/2 cup shortening

1/2 tsp. salt

1 tsp. vanilla

1 cup white sugar

2 eggs, unbeaten

3/4 cup sifted flour

1/2 cup finely chopped walnuts or pecans

Take a drinking glass 2 to 3 inches in diameter, and cover the bottom with a damp towel or cloth. Flatten each cookie with the bottom of the glass. Bake at 325° for 10–15 minutes. Watch the cookies carefully during the last few minutes; because the batter is thin, they can burn easily. Remove from the baking sheet and cool on racks. This recipe will make about 30 yummy chocolate cookies.

Robert Louis Stevenson Oatmeal Cookies

1 cup shortening (can be half butter)
1 cup brown sugar
1 cup white sugar
2 eggs, beaten
1 tsp. vanilla
1-1/2 cups flour
1 tsp. salt
1 tsp. baking soda
3 cups uncooked oatmeal (do not use instant)
1/2 cup chopped walnuts (optional)

A honeymoon spent in an abandoned mine bunkhouse is not for everyone, but Robert and Fanny Stevenson found it an exhilarating experience. Stevenson's book *Silverado Squatters* is about their life in a deserted mining village on Mt. St. Helena, and is classic California reading. Today a marble tablet memorializes the site of Stevenson's cabin.

Stevenson's domestic duties for the morning included starting the fire in the stove for oatmeal and coffee. As a Scot, he had a passion for oatmeal. In tribute to this beloved author, wine country picnics often include oatmeal cookies.

This is an icebox cookie, in that the dough is made ahead and chilled, then sliced and baked as the cookies are needed.

Cream the shortening and sugar together until light and fluffy. Add eggs and vanilla, and blend into a creamy mixture. Sift the dry ingredients together and add to the mixture in the bowl. Mix well. Stir in the oatmeal and nuts.

When well mixed, shape into rolls of desired diameter. Wrap in waxed paper and chill at least four hours. The dough will keep up to a week in the refrigerator, or longer in the freezer. When you are ready to bake the cookies, slice the dough into 1/4″ slices with a sharp knife. Bake on an ungreased cookie sheet for 10 minutes at 350°. The cookies should be a nice golden brown. Remove from sheet and cool on rack. This will make 4 to 5 dozen cookies.

Garden Club Cheese Cake Cookies

I have been a member of the Hermosa Garden Club for over two decades. Our members help many state conservation projects and beautify our city. This cookie is always a popular one for our lunches because it needs no molding, chilling, or other fussy details.

Crust

1/3 cup butter

1/3 cup brown sugar

1 cup sifted all-purpose flour

1/2 cup chopped nuts

Cream butter and brown sugar together until light and fluffy. Add flour and nuts. Blend until mixture resembles crumbs. Remove and set aside one cup. Press remaining dough into a 9″ square pan and bake at 350° for 12 minutes.

While the crust is baking combine the following:

1 8-oz. pkg. cream cheese (room temperature)

1/4 cup granulated sugar

1 egg, slightly beaten

2 T. milk

1 T. fresh lemon juice

1/2 tsp. vanilla

Beat sugar and cream cheese together until smooth. Add egg, milk, lemon juice, and vanilla. Beat until well blended.

Remove crust from oven. Let rest a few minutes, then carefully spread the cream cheese mixture over the crust. Top with the reserved crust mixture. Return to oven and bake at 350° for another 25 minutes. Cool pan on rack. Cut into squares or bars.

Drinks

Punches, Cocktail Favorites, and Wines

Drinking wine with dinner has been a tradition in California since the days of the Spanish fiestas. Today, California wines are world famous, and their production is one of the most important industries of the state. Vineyards make an ecological preserve of thousand of acres of superb prime land. The valleys of Napa and Sonoma offer some of the most beautiful sights in America.

My mother and father were of an era where cocktails were always served before dinner, usually highballs. In the later years of her life, my grandmother would have a sip of sherry before meals, or sometimes brandy. By then, she felt it was a healthy thing to do as she had a heart difficulty. She would tell me how much better she felt after her sip of sherry or brandy. For some time now, the popular trend in California has been to drink wine rather than hard liquor. California drinkers tend to be responsible and have responded well to the idea of the designated driver. Mineral waters are much in favor, as well.

Punches and sangria are often served at brunches and parties. For special celebrations, champagne is always the number one choice.

Californians love coffee. There are many high-quality coffee bars and counters all around the state. Herb and regular teas are offered in most restaurants. There is a drink for everyone in California.

California Martini

A cocktail historian at the *Los Angeles Times* says that the martini was first created over a century ago by a bartender in the small town of Martinez, north of San Francisco. This town was named after a former San Francisco mayor. There have always been opinions and sometimes heated arguments about the perfect martini. This is reputedly the uncomplicated original recipe:

Stir gin and vermouth together. Pour into a chilled cocktail glass containing a green olive. This will make one martini.

2 oz. gin
Dry vermouth to taste
green olive

That "to taste" isn't very helpful, if you're trying to make a martini for someone else. Originally, equal amounts of gin and vermouth were used. Over the years, the martini has gotten "dryer" (less vermouth). The traditional formula is 3 parts gin to 1 part vermouth, but many now prefer it with 5 or even 8 parts gin to 1 part vermouth. Just remember, the dryer it is wanted, the less vermouth you should use.

Orange Sangria

Sangria is popular for brunches and patio parties. The orange juice reflects California's passion for oranges. This is colorful and very refreshing.

1-1/2 cups fresh orange juice

1/2 cup sugar

2 oranges, unpeeled, thinly sliced

1 lime, unpeeled, thinly sliced

1 red apple, diced, with skin left on for color

1/2 gallon of either dry red wine or dry white wine

Simmer the orange juice and sugar together for 5 minutes to make a light syrup. Cool, then add oranges, lime, and apple. Add the wine. Refrigerate for up to a day.

To serve, fill a pitcher with ice and add sangria. This sangria can also be heated and served hot if the weather is wintry and cold. This will serve 8.

White Sangria

This is a sangria variation using white wine. It is very attractive and rather elegant.

about 3 cups sliced fruits of your choice: peaches, honeydew melon slices, etc.

1 lemon and 1 orange, unpeeled, cut in thin slices

1/2 cup sugar

1 bottle (750 ml) dry white wine

1 6-oz. bottle club soda

Combine fruit with sugar and wine. Cover and refrigerate at least an hour or overnight. To serve, add the club soda to the wine and fruit mixture and place in a pitcher with ice. This will serve 4–5.

Linda's California Orange Champagne

My niece Linda uses this combination for her brunch entertaining. It looks pretty and goes perfectly with brunch menus.

orange juice

champagne

fresh strawberries

Combine equal amounts of fresh orange juice with champagne. Serve in a glass garnished with a fresh strawberry.

Cold Duck

In the sixties and seventies, the supermarkets were selling a sickly sweet champagne mixture called "Cold Duck." Fortunately, their customers did not like it. The true cold duck originated in Germany and is lovely.

2 T. lemon juice

4 T. sugar

peel of one large lemon

2 bottles (750 ml) of Rhine or Moselle wine, chilled

1 bottle of dry white champagne, chilled

Combine the lemon juice and sugar in a glass punch bowl. Stir until the sugar dissolves. Make the "duck" by cutting the peel off a large lemon in a continuous strip from the top to the bottom of the lemon, keeping the strip attached to the bottom of the lemon. Place the top of the strip over the lip of the punch bowl and the "body" in the bowl. Pour the wine and champagne into the bowl and blend. This will make enough to fill 24 small punch glasses.

Kir

California visitors to France brought Kir back home with them. Kir is a predinner drink, a simple combination of cassis syrup mixed with white wine. The color is lovely, and the cassis flavor combined with wine is a flawless combination. Cassis may be purchased in most liquor stores.

> *1/2 oz. cassis syrup*
> *5 oz. chilled white wine*

This makes one serving. I usually do not measure the ingredients as this is a rather casual recipe. You may simply pour the cassis in a glass and add the wine. As the heavier cassis diffuses in the white wine, it makes a nice graduated effect.

Bagdad by the Bay

This San Francisco drink is a popular favorite in the city. It has a great citrus-rum flavor.

> *1-1/4 oz. rum*
> *1-1/4 oz. Galliano liqueur*
> *5 oz. fresh chilled orange juice*
> *orange and lime slices for garnish*

Pour rum and Galliano over ice cubes in a large champagne-style glass. Add orange juice and stir. Garnish with orange and lime slices. This makes one "Bagdad."

Irish Coffee

The finest Irish coffee in the state is to be had at Buena Vista in San Francisco (the corner of Hyde and Beach streets). This is where Irish coffee was first served in California. Stanton Delaplane, a travel writer, brought this drink recipe to Buena Vista from the Shannon Airport in Ireland. Perhaps one of the finest experiences to be had in California is that of sipping an Irish coffee at Buena Vista on a foggy night. Of course, you can also make it at home. It is a terrific ending for a dinner.

For each drink use:

1 jigger Irish whiskey (1-1/4 oz.)
2 sugar cubes
good strong coffee
slightly sweetened whipping cream

Pour the whiskey into a warmed glass. Add the sugar cubes and then the hot coffee. To avoid possible breakage of the glass, pour hot coffee over a metal spoon in the glass. Stir well. Float the cream on top of the coffee by pouring it over the back of a teaspoon. The result should be a dark hot coffee mixture topped by a band of white cream. When you take a sip you will be drinking hot coffee through the cool white cream. Please use only real whipping cream. It should be whipped just until thick, but not stiff.

Sunset Cooler Punch
(Non-alcoholic)

It is always important at large parties to provide a punch that is without alcohol for children, and adults with dietary concerns. This sunset-colored punch is cooling and flavorful.

1 cup orange juice

1/2 cup lemon juice

1 cup pineapple juice

1 bottle (1 liter) ginger ale

ice cubes

mint sprigs or a few slices of fresh fruit or strawberries for garnish

Combine all ingredients in a bowl. Garnish with a few mint sprigs. This will serve 4. The recipe may be doubled, tripled, or otherwise increased for large groups.

Classic Mexican Margarita

Margaritas are a bar favorite all over California. Often they are served as doubles in oversized glasses. Margaritas are the perfect beginning for a Mexican dinner. This is the basic, classic recipe.

lime wedge

salt

1-1/2 oz. tequila

3/4 oz. orange liqueur

1-1/2 T. lime juice (fresh preferred)

crushed ice

Take the lime wedge and rub it around the rim of a medium sized glass or goblet. Place a layer of salt on a saucer. Rub the glass rim in salt to coat edge. Combine tequila, orange liqueur, and lime juice. Mix well. Add ice, and mix or shake well. Pour into glass. This makes one margarita.

Raspberry Punch

This is a light, lovely punch that is appropriate for bridal showers, ladies' luncheons, or even a Christmas party.

> *1 box frozen raspberries (10 or 12 oz.),*
> *   or 1 to 1-1/2 cups fresh*
> *1 bottle (750 ml) of dry white wine,*
> *   chilled*
> *1 bottle of chilled champagne*

Combine raspberries with the champagne and wine in a punch bowl. Stir gently and serve to 6.

Hermosa Beach Summer Punch

We love summer picnics in Hermosa Beach My friends have used this punch recipe for many years. It is goes well with any picnic food.

> *dry white wine*
> *ginger ale*
> *lemon slices*

Combine equal amounts of ginger ale and white wine. Add one lemon slice per portion. The amount of each to be used will depend on the amount of people to be served.

Orange Raja

This celebrated holiday hot drink is of European origin, but it combines two of our California treasures, oranges and red wine. The flavor is robust and marvelous.

> *1 cup of sugar*
> *4 oranges*
> *1 quart dry red wine*

Roast the oranges: cut in slices crossways (unpeeled) and place in a baking dish in one layer. Bake at 300° about 20 minutes—just until they turn light brown. Remove from pan. Place in a glass or stainless steel bowl. Cover with the sugar and 2 cups of the wine. Stir well. Cover and keep in a cool place for 24 hours.

To serve, strain the mixture into a large saucepan. Press orange slices in the strainer to remove juice. Add the remaining wine and heat the mixture. This will serve 4, but can easily be doubled or tripled as needed.

Winter Grog

Skiing is a popular sport in California's mountains, and after skiing, grog is the perfect drink for a warming spirit.

> *1 jigger of rum (light or dark)*
> *1 tsp. sugar*
> *hot water to fill the glass*
> *slice of lemon*

Pour the rum and sugar into the glass. Add the hot water and lemon. Stir well and serve at once.

Index

INDEX